POSITIVE AFRICAN AMERICAN MEN-UNITED

A Cultural Revolution
Establishing
The One Code of Honor for Men
and
Master Plan of Action for African American People

By Sidney Wingfield, M.S.S.W.

First Edition

African American Positive Press, Nashville, Tennessee

POSITIVE AFRICAN AMERICAN MEN-UNITED

A Cultural Revolution
Establishing
The One Code of Honor for Men
and
Master Plan of Action for African American People

By Sidney Wingfield, M.S.S.W.

Published By: African American Positive Press
Post Office Box 80491
Nashville, TN 37208-80491

All Rights Reserved
No Part of this book may be used or reproduced without written permission.
Copyright © 1993, 1991 by Sidney Wingfield, M.S.S.W.

First Edition

Printed in the United States of America

Library of Congress Catalog Card Number
93-07312

ISBN 1-883874-49-1 soft cover

FOREWORD

African American Unity Prayer

Our Creator
we pray for unity
under the direction of your spirit and will,
to work, think and act in a positive way.
To honor, respect and protect
our women, children, elders and men
through our love, commitment, guidance,
time and support.

We pray
that you lead us in promoting sincere brotherhood
by our proudly befriending and standing
shoulder to shoulder
with the positive people of
our race and the world.

Amen.

We ask that all African American gatherings of two or more recite this prayer at the beginning of each meeting, until we are united.

POSITIVE AFRICAN AMERICAN MEN-UNITED

MISSION STATEMENT

I. TO RAISE GENERATIONS OF CHILDREN WHO ARE HEALTHY, POLITE, WELL-MANNERED AND REFLECT HOME TRAINING IN THEIR ATTITUDE AND BEHAVIOR.

II. TO DEVELOP OUR CHILDREN INTO POSITIVE MEN AND WOMEN WHO HONORABLY CONTRIBUTE TO THEMSELVES AND THE WORLD.

III. TO ENCOURAGE, TRAIN AND SUPPORT OUR POSITIVE MEN AND WOMEN TO RELATE AND INTERACT WITH EACH OTHER AS LADIES AND GENTLEMEN.

Proverbs 22:06

Train up a child in the way he should go, and when he is old he will not depart from it.

Positive African American Men-United For Generations To Come

PHILOSOPHY

The eight philosophies are written to give balance to The One Code of Honor for men and The Master Plan of Action. All action taken should be in harmony with the eight philosophies.

1. Each and every person is born with natural God given talent and ability, that if discovered and developed will allow that person to earn an honest living.

2. It is the responsibility of African American men to create and maintain an atmosphere conducive for the positive development and realization of our races talents and abilities.

3. Only African American men can define the standard by which they are judged as men.

4. Men can only be held responsible for or judged by those areas upon which they have power, control or influence.

5. The responsibility for a man's race and family cannot be delegated.

6. No man is obligated to do more or less than the best he can do, and only he and God can judge this.

7. No male can mentally separate himself from God or attempt to live separate from God, and at the same time gain, maintain, or sustain true manhood.

8. Only in and with the spirit of unselfish love, and the blessing of God can any of our efforts truly be meaningful and successful.

THE ONE CODE OF HONOR FOR MEN AND THE MASTER PLAN OF ACTION

I. The One Code of Honor for Men:

1. Provides one unifying, objective definition of manhood that can be passed from generation to generation.

2. Is based on the traditional African and African American values of:
   a. God first
   b. positive thoughts and action
   c. duty
   d. family priorities
   e. responsibilities
   f. brotherhood

3. Has been translated and illustrated into universal symbols for easy and simple communication, teaching and learning. This illustration is also used as our logo and named "The Star of Man."

4. Is the unifying element and value base for the Master Plan of Action.

5. Provides a value system that can be used by every one regardless of religious, political, economic or social status.

II. The Master Plan of Action consists of five points of light shining on Ten Places for Action. The Five Points of Light represent five areas for training and participation. The Ten Places for Action represent places in our society, where the training needs to be implemented and practiced.

The Five Points of Light are:
1. The Seven Rites of Passage
2. The Family contract
3. The Tutoring Train
4. The Mentorship Programs
5. Conflict Resolution, Mediation, Organization and Leadership Training

The Ten Places for Action are:
1. The Family
2. Our Elders
3. Religious institutions and organizations
4. Health care and educational systems
5. Correctional systems/Chemical Dependency
6. Helping professions, business, science, art
7. Veterans, Unions, fraternities, sororities, social clubs
8. Community centers, sports, recreation
9. African American Recognition and unity month (Black History Month renamed and Rededicated)
10. The African American National Institute of Achievement and Culture

TABLE OF CONTENTS

TABLE OF CONTENTS

	FOREWORD-Unity Prayer	iii
	Mission Statement	iv
	Philosophy	v
	Outline: The One Code of Honor For Men And The Master Plan Of Action	vi
I.	**INTRODUCTION**-In God We Trust	1
	Preface, Dedication and Acknowledgements	2
	Introduction	3
	The Missing Pieces to the Puzzle	3
	Historical View	3
	The Problem	4
	The Cultural Revolution	5
	To the Men	6
II.	**THE ONE CODE OF HONOR FOR MEN**	9
	Overview-The One Code of Honor for Men	10
	Principles Outlined	10
	The Pledge	12
	Three Age Groups	12
	Code of Honor and Pledge - Men	13
	Code of Honor and Pledge - Teen Men Ages 12-17	14
	Code of Honor and Pledge - Young Men Ages 4-11	15
	Instructions - Men	16
	Instructions - Teen Men Ages 12-17	18
	Instructions - Young Men Ages 4-11	19
III.	**THE STAR OF MAN**	20
	The Star of Man	21
	Illustration I	23, 25
	Principles in Symbol Form	24
	The Golden Spears of Positive Thought and Action	26
IV.	**THE MASTER PLAN OF ACTION FOR AFRICAN AMERICAN PEOPLE**	27
	The Master Plan of Action: A Cultural Revolution	28
	Love and Positive Reinforcement as the Number One Working Tool	29
	Positive Reinforcement	29
	Love	29
	Policy of Confidentiality	30

The Five Points of Light 31
Point of Light #1: Seven Rites of Passage 32
Men's Week 35
Point of Light #2: The Family Contract 36
The Code of Honor as Family Contract 37
        Ages 4-11 Contract 38
        Ages 4-11 Contract (sample) 40
        Ages 12-17 Contract 42
Point of Light #3: The Tutoring Train 44
Each One-Teach One 44
Timing 46
Point of Light #4: Mentorship Program 47
Each One, Reach One-Definition 47
Basic Mentorship Tools 47
Honesty As A Working Tool 48
Schools 49
Team Approach 49
Programs 49
Other Considerations 50
Adult Mentorship 50
Point of Light #5: Conflict Resolution, Mediation, Organization
    and Leadership Training 51
The Ten Places For Action 53
Action Area #1: The Family 54
        "Pride" Parents Small Group or Team 57
Action Area #2: Our Elders 59
Action Area #3: Religious Institutions and Organizations 61
Action Area #4: Health Care Systems and Educational Systems 63
Action Area #5: Correctional Systems/Chemical Dependency 68
Action Area #6: Helping Professionals, Business, Science and Art 70
Action Area #7: Veterans, Unions, Fraternities, Sororities, and Social Clubs 71
Action Area #8: Community, Community Centers, Sports, and Recreation 72
Action Area #9: African American Recognition and Unity Month (AARUM) 75
Action Area #10: The African American National Institute of
    Achievement and Culture 79

V. **ORGANIZATIONAL INFORMATION** 80
Organizational Information: Positive African American Men-United, Inc. 81
Classification 81
Purpose 81
Mission 81
Goals 82
Policy of Unity Above Politics and Religion 83
Honor System 83
Member, Participant, Supporter, Patron 84
Dues and Registration Costs 85
Coverage 85

	Affiliation Requirement	86
	What You Can Do: Local and Community Level	86
	Power and Control - Executive Committee/Advisory Board	86
	Funding	88
	Strategy and Implementation Plan	89
	Membership Application	90
VI.	**NOTES AND VISIONS**	91
	To The African American Woman	92
	What About Our Girls and Young Women - The Unspoken Problem	94
	The Traditional African American Church - The Exception and the Rule	95
	African American Unity Prayer	97
	Brotherhood	97
	Note from the Klan	98
	The Oppressor/The Enemy-Ignorance, Fear, Indifference, and Disunity	99
	Dialogue With White America	100
	A Special Note to the White Woman's Liberation Movement	102
	To The Hispanic Communities	103
	To The Asian Pacific American Communities and People	103
	To The American Jewish People	104
	To The Native American	104
	To Our African Brothers and Sisters	105
	America's Chosen People	106
	We Are African European Americans: The Hard and Painful Truth	106
	The Elderly	110
	The Greatest Outrage	111
	Jobs and Unemployment	112
	Sisters and Brothers Without Fathers or Mothers	113
VII.	**TERMS**	114
VIII.	**ABOUT THE AUTHOR**	118

I

INTRODUCTION

"In God We Trust"

Positive African American Men-United will use the term "God" throughout our cultural revolution as our foundation for faith. We define and use this term in the exact context and wisdom as the Founding Fathers of the United States of America did, in their creation of our Constitution and Monetary System.

The belief and trust in God as a foundation of faith are the history, heritage and future of African American people. No lasting values, culture or country can be seriously built and indefinitely maintained without a foundation of faith based on the greatest power known to humanity: Trust In God.

PREFACE, DEDICATION AND ACKNOWLEDGMENTS

I thank God the Creator of all that is or ever will be. I thank God the ultimate infinite reality for its love, mercy, compassion, wisdom, and order.

I give thanks for an opportunity to grow and know God's love through His expression in me. I give thanks for an opportunity to be used in a positive manner, in the next progressive step of my race, culture, and people.

I pray and ask for protection and guidance to know the meaningful things I do, say, and write can be God's expression through me.

This book is primarily dedicated to my Creator. Second, it is dedicated to my foster parents William and Sarah Bass, my grandfather Judge Randolph Wingfield, and my natural father Plato Barnett, all of whom are deceased. Third, it is dedicated to all victims of oppression and ignorance who have given their lives to see the human race progress and grow closer to God and knowledge. Fourth, it is dedicated to all the infinite generations to come. Finally, I dedicate this book to the positive humans who seek a vehicle for expression and change toward the positive.

My thanks and appreciation are given to the numerous people who have helped and supported me with this work.

With God All Things Are Possible

INTRODUCTION

The Missing Pieces to the Puzzle

The purpose of this book is to provide African American people with the working tools needed to take our next developmental step forward as a united race and culture.

The missing pieces to the puzzle of our people are that:

1. **We have not created a culture or society based on principles which work for us.**

2. **We lack unity across sexual, social, political, economic, and religious lines.**

3. **The men of our race have not yet defined themselves in a way that can be passed from generation to generation.**

This book provides a unifying definition of true manhood formed in The One Code of Honor for men. The Code of Honor can easily be passed from generation to generation. The Master Plan of Action in this work gives the blue print, working tools, and material to build our culture.

Historical View

From the beginning and throughout the existence of humanity, certain traits, characteristics, and values have been common to all peoples and cultures. Examples of common traits and characteristics are laughter and tears to all people, music and dance to all cultures. Just as common and universal as laughter, tears, music and dance are to all peoples and cultures, also certain cultural base values are common.

Historically each and every culture that has existed and prospered has held three values; these values are self determination, responsibility, and unity. This first value of self determination is simply that the men of a particular race or culture collectively define their own manhood and collectively pass this definition from generation to generation. The second value is that the men of this race are responsible for the guidance, care, and protection of their elderly, women, and children. The third value is that the men of the race or culture are to stand united to insure the existence, safety, and well being of their race or culture. Historically, no race or culture of men can delegate these responsibilities and, at the same time, maintain respect or progress that race forward. This has been proven as factual as the universal law of gravity on earth. The African American people are the only group of people on the face of the earth who lack a culture and history based on the wisdom of the founding fathers and elders of that race.

For those who may be fearful of compromising their religious belief, remember that every religion known to man has been built around and integrated into the existing culture and history of that people. Jesus' ministry was originally directed towards the Jewish Hebrew culture and religion. Muhammad's original message was for the establishment of unity in his culture around The Belief in The One God. There is no religion that exists in a vacuum. All religions rest on the culture of the people who practice that religion. It can be said that culture is to religion what wheels are to a car.

The Problem

The first problem and task African American men face, in relationship to self determination, is the establishment of an honest, true, and attainable definition of manhood.

The current 500 year old definition of "Free, White, and 21," is for obvious reasons unattainable and psychologically damaging to our entire race. Accompanying the above definition of manhood is the unspoken and sometimes unrecognized attitude of might is right, and white is might.

If you can't name it you can't claim it. No objective definition of African American manhood exists today. If you ask 100 African American men to define manhood you will get 100 different answers. It is no wonder our youth are confused when their elders have failed to give them a collective united working definition of what it means to be a man. **Until we define manhood we can not teach it**.

The second problem we face as a minority is that the dominant culture has historically assumed responsibility for our elderly, women, and children through politics, economics, and passive religious teachings, taken out of context. As victims of oppression and people of color, we face realities over which we have no control, but we do have positive options we have not used until now. We must, with a positive attitude, face the reality that we cannot fully assimilate, dominate, or separate from this society.

The Cultural Revolution

The term cultural revolution is not intended to encourage or activate any type of physical violence or destruction. The cultural revolution is a mental cultural and ideological offensive. The cultural revolution is a turning over of African American mental soil for spring time planting in the rich earth of our foreparents' sacrifices. The cultural revolution is the seed planting of old values with new ideas and visions to produce unity, prosperity, and peace for all African American people and communities.

No true progress can be made or unity achieved until we establish the ground rules for our people and enforce them.

The Code of Honor for men is a collection of the values African Americans have affirmed and requested as their cultural base. The Code of Honor for men is inclusive of the positive elements of every culture and society that has maintained its existence and prospered. The Master Plan of Action is based on the values of The Code of Honor. This plan consists of five points of light, to be shined on ten places for action. The five points of light represent specific areas for education, training, and participation of our entire race and culture. The ten places for action represent primary places in our society where our education, training, and participation need to be implemented and practiced. The Master Plan of Action gives African American people a thorough and complete overlapping basket weave network to cover and care for our entire race.

Above and beyond The One Code of Honor for men, as the foundation for African American Cultural Revolution, it is a model for those who oppress the world to find liberation from the chains of their own oppression.

The time has come for each individual to assume responsibility as part of the solution or part of the problem. The dividing line is your willingness to unite, and to place your people ahead of your personal agendas for the sake of unity.

To The Men

The cultural revolution requires men of courage and integrity to accept responsibility for the guidance, care, and protection of our elderly, women, and children. It is built with the cement of respect for ourselves, our elders, women, and children.

Before we can receive respect, we must first deserve it. No man who shirks his responsibility and refuses to give what he has to offer to his people can be respected.

As a minority race, people of color, and victims of oppression, African Americans have less economic, political, and assertive religious power. **But no system of oppression can limit the amount of love, knowledge, and spirituality we possess and pass on to our children, through our time and commitment.**

We African American men who are positive must unite and agree upon a Code of Honor that can be passed from generation to generation, as a definition of African American manhood. If we cannot agree and unite on the value of God, family, positive thought, positive action, and brotherhood, what can we agree on? What can we unite around?

The last great movement of our people was the Civil Rights struggle. This was based on a reaction to injustice and our attack was from a passive-aggressive strategy. Conditions now warrant a cultural offensive with an active aggressive strategy.

Our women have done more than their share and carried the responsibility for our race on their shoulders and breasts. Let us, as men, do what we know we need to do. As men, let us begin at the beginning.

The One Code of Honor for men and Master Plan of Action is a place to begin, with each and every positive African American man committing himself to these values and actions, and passing them on to each of his sons and daughters and to every African American child in his sphere of contact and influence.

Saying what needs to be done is always easier than doing it. Three ingredients are necessary for progress: figuring out what needs to be done, how to do it, and where to begin. This means: analyzation, preparation, and implementation.

The object of Positive African American Men United (PAAM-U) is unity, which is the first principle of Kwanzaa. Positive African American Men United (PAAM-U) seeks to establish unity between all African American men on four principles that are positive and universal:

1. **The belief in the spirit of God within us and the reality of God outside us as the primary cause of existence.**

2. **A commitment for African American men to think and act in a positive way.**

3. **A belief that African American men are the responsible parties for our elders, women, and children.**

4. **The promotion of sincere brotherhood among positive men of our race and the world.**

If we can agree to unite and work together among ourselves, to live and teach these four basic principles in our own individual group, through our own individual religion, we have at hand, the solution to all of the other problems we have attacked directly but in which we have found only limited success or failure. If we cannot unite on at least these four cultural values, our race is doomed to extended suffering and humiliation until a generation is born that will unite. **History has proven there can be no unity or true progress unless the men of the race take their appropriate leadership roles.**

Individual courage and valor exist throughout our history. We can be proud of ourselves. Group unity, courage, and valor is our next step. This step <u>must</u> be taken as an action, not a reaction. Our willingness to sacrifice individual ego and personal agendas for the sake of unity will be the line which divides those who are part of the solution from those who are part of the problem. Our time line for phase one of this program is 21 years.

II

THE ONE CODE OF HONOR

FOR MEN

THE ONE CODE OF HONOR FOR MEN

OVERVIEW

The One Code of Honor For Men

1. Provides one unifying objective definition of manhood that can be passed from generation to generation.

2. Is based on the traditional African and African American values:

   a. God first
   b. Positive thoughts and action
   c. Duty
   d. Family priorities
   e. Responsibilities
   f. Brotherhood

3. Has been translated and illustrated into universal symbols for easy and simple communication, teaching, and learning. This illustration is also used as our logo and named "The Star of Man."

4. Is the unifying element and value base for the Master Plan of Action.

5. Provides a value system that can be used by everyone regardless of religious, political, economic or social status.

Principles Outlined

The One Code of Honor for Men is divided into seven basic parts:

   I. Spiritual Relationship to God
   II. Mental, Positive Thoughts and Actions
   III. Emotional, Family, Values
   IV. Physical, Brotherhood
   V. Honor, Manhood, Responsibility
   VI. Responsibility and Privileges
   VII. Courage and Goals

Part I. Reflects the values of God, spirituality and religion in relation to ourselves and the world outside ourselves. It increases in difficulty, commitment and responsibility from age four to adulthood.

There are some principles which require a family consensus. They are:

1. God first.

2. God as the primary cause of all existence. A part of God exists within each person. This is the source of life, without which life cannot exist. It is called many things--spirit, soul, essence, primary reality, etc. It is this essence of divinity, or God within us, that comes from God and returns to God which is the true reality of our existence.

3. One can study and learn about God, the world, and our relationship between the two.

This first section is the most difficult to learn, understand, and live. It is not intended to be mastered but pursued as the ideal.

Part II Deals with Thoughts and Actions or the Mental Aspect of Man

1. Positive vs. Negative

2. Extremely difficult to learn and master

Part III Tells what a man's duties and responsibilities are: Protection, Respect, Honor

1. Describes to whom these duties and responsibilities (priorities) are directed: Women, Children, Elders, Self, Family, Race

2. The specific vehicles to be used to fulfill these duties and responsibilities: Love, Commitment, Guidance, Support, Time

Part IV   Deals with a commitment to brotherhood with positive men in the race and world. This translates into anti-homicide, anti-war, pro-brotherhood and peace.

The Pledge

The pledge represents the individual's commitment to the Code. One can read and study the Code of Honor, but commitment is required to qualify one as a man.

Part V   Honor Bound - Manhood is responsibility

Part VI   Relationship between privilege and responsibility

Part VII   Courage to face all the barriers and obstacles known to defeat men. It also indirectly implies drugs and alcohol abuse are escapes from unpleasant tasks and are cowardly. What can start as an escape ends in an addiction more powerful and unpleasant than the original tasks.

Three Age Groups

The following pages will reflect three Codes of Honor for three age groups:

1. The One Code of Honor for Men
2. The Teen Code of Honor ages 12 - 17
3. The Young Men's Code of Honor ages 4 - 11

Codes 2 and 3 were designed to be age appropriate, with teaching and training beginning at age 2 when the child begins to speak. The ultimate goal is mastering the one Code of Honor for Men.

THE ONE CODE OF HONOR FOR

MEN

1. It is my duty and responsibility as a man to pursue love, knowledge, and understanding of God's spirit within me and the reality of God as the primary cause of all existence outside of me.

2. It is my duty and responsibility as a man to work, think, and act in a positive way.

3. It is my duty and responsibility as a man to honor, respect, and protect our women, children, elders, and self, through love, commitment, guidance, time, and support.

4. It is my duty and responsibility as a man to promote sincere brotherhood by proudly befriending and standing shoulder to shoulder with the positive men of my race and the world.

THE PLEDGE (Commitment)

5. I pledge my life, to honor this Code, and never use the Code of Honor to willingly or knowingly take advantage, misuse, or abuse those entrusted to my care and protection.

6. I realize and accept the fact of manhood as a responsibility to myself, my family and my people. I understand and accept that my responsibilities as a man may outweigh my privileges.

7. I am courageous, I can face and complete tasks which require hard work, dirty work, and responsibility to care for my people and reach my goals in life.

THE CODE OF HONOR FOR
TEEN MEN - AGES 12-17

1. It is my duty and responsibility as a growing man to observe, listen, and study how God works within me, the world, and the universe.

2. It is my duty and responsibility as a growing man to learn and master positive thought and actions.

3. It is my duty and responsibility as a growing man to learn and master our tradition of honoring, respecting and protecting--our women, children, elders, and self, through love, commitment, guidance, time, and support.

4. It is my duty and responsibility as a growing man to proudly befriend and stand shoulder to shoulder with the positive men of my race and the world.

THE PLEDGE (Commitment)

5. These four codes I am honor-bound to learn and live. I realize and accept the fact of manhood as a responsibility to myself, my family, and my people.

6. I understand that my privileges are based on my willingness to know, accept, and complete my responsibilities at home and in school.

7. I am courageous and can face and complete tasks which require hard work, dirty work, and responsibility to reach my goals and manhood.

THE CODE OF HONOR FOR YOUNG MEN - AGES 4-11

1. It is my duty and responsibility as a young man to learn all I can about God and the world he created.

2. It is my duty and responsibility as a young man to listen and learn at home and in school. Knowledge and Truth are my friends for life.

3. It is my duty and responsibility as a young man to Honor and respect myself, members of my family, and my race.

4. It is my duty and responsibility as a young man to proudly befriend, and stand shoulder to shoulder with the positive young men of my race and the world.

THE PLEDGE (Commitment)

5. These four codes I am honor-bound to learn and live. I realize and accept the fact of manhood as a responsibility to myself, my family, and my people.

6. I understand that my privileges are based on my willingness to accept and complete my responsibilities at home and in school.

7. I have courage to face and complete tasks which require hard work, dirty work, and responsibility to reach my goals and manhood.

INSTRUCTIONS

MEN

PART I

The One Code of Honor for men is extremely challenging. It requires effort and aspiration to the limit of one's being. True manhood is challenging and requires all of one's being.

The pursuit of love, knowledge, and understanding of God's spirit within oneself is the paramount of manhood. It is elusive in that with the attainment of one level, the next level is revealed. This is much like the student who masters addition, subtraction, and multiplication to discover division, algebra, trigonometry and on through quantum mechanics. The point is that as long as we are alive, we can grow and learn in our love, understanding, and knowledge of God within and without.

In business they have an expression, "As long as you're green you're growing, but as soon as you think you're ripe, you turn rotten."

The on-going and continued growth of man spiritually is his primary responsibility that makes all else relatively easy and fall in its proper place. This spiritual responsibility is agreed upon by all religious denominations, sects, wise men, prophets, and spiritual leaders.

PART II

Ye shall judge a tree by the fruit it bears. Positive thought and action is the key to true manhood. As oppressed people, remaining positive in the face of those who deny your right to exist on the planet is challenging, however, our families and children are double victims if we sink to negative thoughts and actions. Our dependents look to, and rightly expect, our leadership and guidance to be positive regardless of our personal hardship. Only positive thought and action can move or progress us forward. Of what value is a man, but to provide, lead, and guide in a positive direction.

PART III

Part III reflects all the attributes incorporated in true man--the principles of protection, respect and honor; the four priorities of those principles: our women, children, elders and self. The five vehicles through which a man can care for his family and people are love, commitment, guidance, time, and support.

To those things you can add to, but none can be taken away.

PART IV

Sincere brotherhood is important. We must work together and with others who are positive to care for the few or the many. Most of all, homicide, the African American male-on-male killing, must stop. The true spirit of the African American male brotherhood must be built in--even as competitors for the same jobs, benefits, and resources which are limited, we must help each other.

INSTRUCTIONS

TEEN MEN - AGES 12-17

The requirements for ages 12 - 17 are more difficult than for ages 4-11 and less difficult than for Men. In the areas of religion and God, the emphasis goes to within the young man, the world, and the universe.

In the area of family, he is pledged to master our tradition of honoring, respecting, and protecting women, children, elders, and self through love, commitment, guidance, support, and time.

Incorporated within these traditions are all of the attributes needed for manhood. We have the principles of honor, respect, and protection. The four priorities are women, children, elders, and self. The five vehicles through which he can care for his people are: love, commitment, guidance, support, and time.

Teen men should exemplify brotherhood in their interactions with other teen men and respect in their interactions with teen women. Conflict resolution and basic respect for teen women should be mastered at this age. Team work, cooperation, and the ability to work and think beyond the latest fad should be a part of this young man's thinking.

African American history is of great importance in this age range. The 12 year old Rite of Passage should include mastery of The Star of Man, complete memorization of the Code of Honor and Pledge, and the recital of one African American man's life and contributions to our culture. Preparation and history of African American culture should begin at age seven and be consistent through the 12th birthday and Rite of Passage.

INSTRUCTIONS

YOUNG MEN - AGES 4-11

Preparation for the ages 4 - 11 Code and Pledge should begin at 2 years of age. During this period the child is learning to speak. The Terms section (in the rear of the book) contains a definition of each word that should be taught. The child should learn the meaning of each sentence and paragraph to the best of his ability to understand.

On the child's fourth birthday a Rite of Passage ceremony to young man status should be held and special presents from friends and relatives should be given with the youth's ability to identify the five principles of The Star of Man. From four to seven, this youth can be asked to repeat the five principles of The Star of Man by any PAAM-U person, but he must also be rewarded for each successful recital. At age seven, preparation for the teen pledge begins (if he is advanced and doing well in all areas), but if there are problems with school, discipline, homework or housework this can be delayed. Most important to remember, no privileges, presents, clothes, or time out is to be granted outside of the Code of Honor and its responsibility. A portion of money should be set aside for a savings account in the youth's name. The parents should determine the percentage to be banked and specific items should be decided for purchase at a specific time, birthday, Christmas, Kwanzaa, etc. Delayed gratification should be learned in this process. The three C's: courtesy, cooperation, and consideration, should be learned and mastered in this age group, and the family contract should be established.

III

THE STAR OF MAN

THE STAR OF MAN

The Star of Man was designed to condense all the principles of the Code of Honor into simple symbolic forms. It also serves a dual function of a logo and teaching tool.

Children at the age of two can learn these symbols as they learn to speak. Each symbol is common and is visible every day in all places. The large Illustration I is to be reproduced on any copy machine and used for coloring with crayons, water colors, or paint. Children and youth should study the meaning of each symbol as they paint with adult or teen supervision. The words on the outside circle provide a teaching tool for spelling and value communication between adult and child. Simple definitions of each word are in the terms section of this book.

The symbols should be learned in order, allowing children to learn how to count to five as they learn the meaning of each symbol.

Number one is the one continuous circle of God within you. This is represented by the small circle in the center of the star. The circle of God outside of you, or without, is represented by the words surrounding the star. Circle of God within is meant to symbolize that spark of divinity, or God, which we call spirit, without which our bodies could be complete and in tact, but life in us still not exist without its presence.

Number two is the two golden spears of positive thought and action which cross behind the star. See Illustration II for information.

Number three is the triangle of duty with each one of the three sides representing a principle or man's duty. These three principles are honor, respect, and protect.

Number four is the square of priorities located inside the star and outside the triangle. Each of the square's four sides represent the priorities in which a man should perform his duties. All four priorities are equal and none should be sacrificed for the other. These priorities are women, children, elders, and self.

Number five is the five pointed Star of Man and his responsibility. It is also called the Star of Man because of its relative shape to a man's body, one head, two arms and two legs. Each point of the star represents one of the primary vehicles, or methods, by which a man fulfills his duty and priority responsibility. These five methods are love, commitment, guidance, time, and support.

Each principal and word contained in the Code of Honor and Star of Man is in print on the outside circle of the logo. We urge parents, teachers, coaches, volunteers, and helping professionals to use the Star of Man as early as possible to teach the values of the Code of Honor. If we start early enough and teach well, our children will have constant reminders of their values every time they see a circle, triangle, star or spear shape, and each time they see the numbers 1, 2, 3, 4, 5.

The Star of Man

ILLUSTRATION.I

POSITIVE AFRICAN AMERICAN MEN - UNITED
THE CODE OF HONOR PRINCIPLES IN SYMBOL FORM
THE STAR OF MAN

1. THE ONE CONTINUOUS CIRCLE OF GOD WITHIN, AND WITHOUT.

2. THE TWO GOLDEN SPEARS OF POSITIVE THOUGHT AND ACTION.

3. THE TRIANGLE OF DUTY: TO HONOR, TO RESPECT AND TO PROTECT.

4. THE SQUARE OF PRIORITIES: OUR WOMEN, CHILDREN, ELDERS, AND SELF.

5. THE FIVE POINTED STAR OF MAN AND HIS RESPONSIBILITY: LOVE, COMMITMENT, GUIDANCE, TIME, AND SUPPORT.

Every star in the heavens is to remind man of his relationship to God and Family.

The Star of Man

ILLUSTRATION.I

THE GOLDEN SPEARS OF POSITIVE THOUGHT AND ACTION

The two Golden Spears of Positive Thought and Action are modeled from the Zulu fighting spear designed by King Shaka Zulu, founder of the South African Zulu Nation. (Born 1787, Died 1828, King 1818-1828). These spears are called Assegai. Every type of Zulu Assegai has a specific name. King Shaka's Assegai was named IXWA pronounced as the click resembling the sound made by a driver urging on his horse.

The Golden Spears of Positive Thought and Action are both defensive and offensive tools and weapons.* The struggle and war against negativity is ongoing and both internal and external. Positive action and thought have been historically victorious over all negative enemies. Every battle may not have been won, but no war has ever been lost.

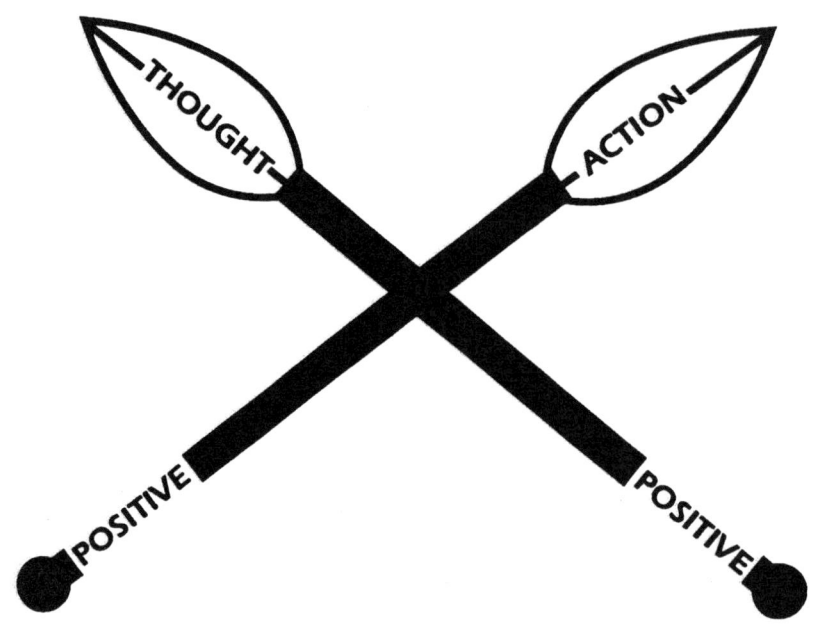

ILLUSTRATION II
*E. A. Ritter, <u>Shaka Zulu</u> (New York: Penguin Books, 1978), pp. 43-46.

IV

THE MASTER PLAN

OF ACTION

FOR

AFRICAN AMERICAN

PEOPLE

THE MASTER PLAN OF ACTION
A CULTURAL REVOLUTION

The Master Plan of Action consists of five points of light shining on Ten Places for Action. The Five Points of Light represent five areas for training and participation. The Ten Places for Action represent places in our society where this training needs to be implemented and practiced.

The Five Points of Light are:

1. The Seven Rites of Passage
2. The Family contract
3. The Tutoring Train
4. The Mentorship Programs
5. Conflict Resolution, Mediation, Organization and Leadership Training

The Ten Places for Action are:

1. The Family
2. Our Elders
3. Religious institutions and organizations
4. Health care, and Educational systems
5. Correctional systems/Chemical Dependency
6. Helping professions, business, science, art
7. Veterans, unions, fraternities, sororities, social clubs
8. Community and community centers, sports, recreation
9. African American Recognition and Unity Month
   (Black History Month Renamed and Rededicated)
10. The African American National Institute of Achievement and Culture

This vision is the first attempt and effort to account for, and communicate with, all of the 30 million African American people in this country. It is my vision that PAAM-U be the answer to the question and the solution to the problem.

Everyone is needed and all positive people can find a level of participation that is tailor-made to their time, money, and talent.

LOVE AND POSITIVE REINFORCEMENT AS THE NUMBER ONE WORKING TOOLS

Love and positive reinforcement are to the Code of Honor and Master Plan of action what cement is to a brick building.

Positive Reinforcement

We must provide positive recognition and reinforcement for every person: child, mother, father, grandparent, uncle, aunt, niece, and nephew for any and all positive attempts, acts or accomplishments no matter how small, minute, or insignificant. **No Good Work, Kind Deed, or Effort should go unnoticed or without praise and reward.**

This one working tool can build more self-esteem and encourage positive behavior in our children and families than any other single element. It is beyond social or economic limits. No matter how wealthy or poor we may be, positive reinforcement can be lavished upon our loved ones and no amount of money can replace its lack.

Love

The ability and capacity to love and express love in a positive way is the most important element of The Master Plan of Action and Code of Honor. Philosophy number seven states: Only in and with the spirit of unselfish love, and the blessing of God can any of our efforts truly be meaningful and successful. **The majority of this entire effort is Love, put into an objective form.** To go through the motions and programs with a motivation less than unselfish love can be more harmful to you and the people you seek to help than if you had done nothing at all.

In the terms section, love is defined as: a level of awareness and concern for another person's well being and progress, beyond your own benefit. The capacity to love must come from your relationship to your God and from your own spirituality. For those who seek to help but have difficulty or concerns in this area please make this known so that our training and education programs can assist you.

Policy of Confidentiality

As we come in contact with members, families and beneficiaries of PAAM-U, we will see and hear many things which are personal and private. We are under oath to protect, respect, and honor the privacy and personal issues of all persons we come in contact with. Rumors, gossip, and betrayal of confidence is unprofessional and a violation of the Code of Honor.

Permission must be obtained from all parties concerned before any personal or private information is shared with another person.

THE FIVE POINTS OF LIGHT

1. **The Seven Rites of Passage**
2. **The Family Contact**
3. **The Tutoring Train**
4. **The Mentorship Programs**
5. **Conflict Resolution, Mediation, Organization and Leadership Training**

The Five Points of Light represent five areas of training and participation. All five points of light (training and education) rest on a value base and philosophy of The Code of Honor. The Code of Honor creates a united and uniform system of cross referencing and education. The use of The Code of Honor as a general frame of reference assists in maintaining discipline and gaining cooperation from all beneficiaries.

The following pages give a basic outline of each point of light. In every step and point of this plan, experienced professionals who can or are willing to learn to communicate across social and economic lines, are encouraged to contribute their expertise and talent.

SEVEN RITES OF PASSAGE: Point of Light #1

The condition of our people does not allow us the luxury of only a token ceremony for manhood. For purposes of comparison, history tells us the Jewish culture has a five thousand (5,000) year old culture base to back them up. Even during their period of slavery in Egypt, their language and culture were maintained. Under the oppression of the Roman empire they maintained their culture and language. Jews were exempt from military draft by Romans because they refused to fight or work on the Sabbath, as their religion dictated.

African Americans have only been out of slavery one second on the world clock. Our mentorship programs, Rites of Passage, and cultural establishment must be pragmatic and continue until we produce a generation of men who are positive and uncompromising with negative thought and action.

The Seven Rites of Passage are the most complete possibility for raising our youth into manhood. All Seven Rites are recommended. The following material gives each parent, guardian, or mentor a value system, working tools, and suggestions for group or individual assistance. All specific aspects of each ceremony should be agreed upon by parents.

The first four Rites are the most important. Until age seven, the child is basically absorbing what he is exposed to. At the age of seven the child will basically have formed his personality and values. After the age of seven, you begin to work on trying to undo negative behavior and replace it with positive behavior.

Each parent must choose the values they wish their child to exhibit as an adult. Parents must begin to teach those values at birth.

I. <u>Birth</u>: The child (male and female rite) is claimed by a positive African American man as our men's responsibility, to love, protect and mentor for the glory of God (Higher Power), our race and humanity. If possible, this Rite should be done at the hospital in the delivery room, but no later than seven days after birth.

II. <u>Two Years Old</u>: The child is introduced to the Star of Man and the symbolism of the circle, spears, triangle, square, and star. The child begins to learn the meaning of words and responsibility of the 4-11 year-old Code of Honor and Pledge.

III. <u>Four Years Old</u>: The child passes to young man status and is formally bound to the Seven Step Code of Honor and Pledge for the 4-11 years old. He is introduced to responsibility in the home which should include taking care of his own toys, dirty clothes, room and/or bed. The young man should be able to point out each symbol of the Star of Man and with assistance make some connection to each principle.

IV. <u>Seven Years Old</u>: The young man is introduced to, and begins a study of, the Teen Men Code of Honor and Pledge. The young man begins study of a parent approved African American History Curriculum. The young man is required to assume additional responsibility in the home, one extracurricular activity after school, and an agreed upon grade point average in school. All rights and privileges are to be based on the home, contract, Code of Honor, and Pledge. He formally begins to academically tutor children ages 2-5, and to teach the principles of the Star of Man and Code of Honor.

V. <u>Eleven Years Old</u>: The young man passes to the status of teen man and is bound to the Code of Honor and Pledge for the 12-17 year-old in a formal ceremony. His contract is revised for more privileges and responsibilities. History of the child's chosen African American role model or hero is recited and interpreted. The five principles within the Star of Man should be recited by memory. He may now tutor and teach ages 2-9.

VI. <u>Fifteen Years Old</u>: The teen man is introduced to the adult Code of Honor and Pledge. The contract, privileges, and responsibilities are renegotiated and signed. He may now tutor and teach ages 2-13.

VII. <u>Eighteen Years Old and Older</u>: The man is bound to the One Code of Honor for Men with full rights and responsibilities of adult manhood. The Star of Man, Code of Honor, and Pledge should have been committed to memory. Each man is officially qualified to teach the Code and Star of Man, to all ages.

Wisdom-Teaching Of Our Elders:

*It is wise to seek and work toward
win-win solutions
for all parties involved.*

MEN'S WEEK

PAAM-U is designating the last seven days of February as Men's Week. During these seven days, all men from all categories will start or renew their pledge to the Code of Honor. During Men's Week all official Rites of Passage may be performed.

Communication of positive achievements of African American men and the intelligent dismantling of negative myths and stereotypes are to be approached openly and publicly in a positive educational manner.

The Seven Rites of Passage have two possible times of year they may be performed: the first on the male's birthday, the second for all males of all ages once a year during Men's Week. It is the responsibility of each man and parent to plan which ceremony they will participate in. It is the responsibility of each community, church, and African American organization to ensure all males in their respective groups have stood up and been counted as honor-bound men.

Wisdom-Teaching Of Our Elders:

*A man automatically obligates himself to
help and improve
that which he criticizes or condemns.*

THE FAMILY CONTRACT: Point of Light #2

The family contract is based on the Code of Honor for young men or teens, and three basic principles which are the starting points of behavior called The 3 C's: **courtesy**, **consideration**, and **cooperation**.

1. **Courtesy**: Positive or good manners shown to all people by words and actions. Example: Please and Thank You, Yes sir, No ma'am, May I go outside and play? Mother, can I stay out late?

2. **Consideration**: Thinking of other people's feelings before you speak or act, with the intent of always trying to help make things better and never to hurt others or make things worse.

3. **Cooperation**: 1. Teamwork, 2. Working, thinking, acting, planning together, sometimes with the leadership instruction or guidance of parents or adults for the achievement of a goal.

The family contract covers each youth's behavior attitude and responsibilities in five basic areas: home, school, community, church, and part time employment. The parents have the option of an oral or written contract. Each aspect of The Code of Honor, 3 C's, and five basic areas should be negotiated with clear understanding of the meanings of each word or term to the best of the youth's ability to understand.

This contract represents the center of all meaningful efforts by parents, teachers, youth workers, ministers, employers, volunteers, and concerned parties. All parties are encouraged to recommend to parents the use of the family contract and facilitate arrangements.

The Code of Honor as Family Contract

The upcoming generation of youth who are raised from birth by responsible PAAM-U members and participants will easily adjust to using the 3C's and contract. The initiation of our present generation to the family contract should be done in harmony with the Seven Rites of passage, tutoring, mentorship, and conflict resolution training.

The age appropriate Code of Honor represents the base and foundation of the family contract. The age to begin is two years old or when the child begins to talk. By the time the child is four he should know and understand every word and term used to the best of their ability. Parents should center discipline and privileges around this Code. If parents do not live together, each household should center discipline and privileges around this Code.

The Code of Honor is intended to be used every day. It is the foundation for privileges and discipline in the home and represents a contract between parents.

Each child's responsibility is clear on all general areas of religion, home, and school. Specifically, he is also held responsible to foster positive brotherhood (anti-homicide) and to respect women. He is held accountable for a positive attitude and behavior. Parents should fill in responsibilities with specific tasks and standards. Examples of this would include making beds, washing dishes, emptying garbage, mopping floors, vacuuming, washing windows, cutting grass, raking leaves, cooking, etc. Specific tasks at school are good behavior, specific grade expectations (A's, B's, C's). Examples of specific spiritual responsibilities are regular church/temple or Sunday school attendance, reading the Bible or Koran, and the study of different religions in the encyclopedia or library. All requirements should depend on the child's ability, and be both fair and reasonable.

The Code of Honor Family Contract
Ages 4-11

I _____ understand and agree this family contract will govern my behavior attitude and responsibility in the following areas: home, school, community church, and part-time employment. The three C's of Courtesy, Consideration and Cooperation are to be used at all times in all places.

RELIGION / CHURCH / TEMPLE / SPIRITUAL EDUCATION
I.   It is my duty and responsibility as a young man to learn all I can about God and the world he created.

    Parent-Guardian: I will _____

    Youth: I will _____

    _____

RESPONSIBILITY AT HOME AND IN SCHOOL
II.   It is my duty and responsibility as a young man to listen and learn at home and in school. Knowledge and Truth are my friends for life.

    Parent-Guardian: I will _____

    Youth: I will _____

    _____

RELATIONSHIP TO FAMILY, SELF, AND COMMUNITY
III.   It is my duty and responsibility as a young man to Honor and respect myself, members of my family, and my race.

    Parent-Guardian: I will _____

    Youth: I will _____

    _____

BROTHERHOOD / COMMUNITY / SCHOOL
IV.   It is my duty and responsibility to proudly befriend, and stand shoulder to shoulder with the positive young men of my race and the world.

    Parent-Guardian: I will _____

    Youth: I will _____

    _____

Ages 4-11

HONOR MANHOOD RESPONSIBILITIES

V. These four codes I am honor bound to learn and live. I realize and accept the fact of manhood as a responsibility to myself, my family, and my people.

Parent-Guardian: I will _____

Youth: I will _____

_____

PRIVILEGES AND RESPONSIBILITY

VI. I understand that my privileges are based on my willingness to accept and complete my responsibilities at home and in school.

Parent-Guardian: I will _____

Youth: I will _____

_____

COURAGE, HARD WORK, DIRTY WORK, GOALS

VII. I have courage to face and complete tasks which require hard work, dirty work, and the responsibility to reach my goals and manhood.

Parent-Guardian: I will _____

Youth: I will _____

_____

Special agreements or understandings

_____

_____

_____

Youth _____ Date From _____ Date To _____

Parent-Guardian _____ Date From _____ Date To _____

The Code of Honor Family Contract
Ages 4-11

I <u> William B. Wingfield </u> understand and agree this family contract will govern my behavior attitude and responsibility in the following areas: home, school, community church, and part-time employment. The three C's of Courtesy, Consideration and Cooperation are to be used at all times in all places.

RELIGION / CHURCH / TEMPLE / SPIRITUAL EDUCATION
I. It is my duty and responsibility as a young man to learn all I can about God and the world he created.

    Parent-Guardian: I will <u>have clean clothes ready for you and transportation.</u>

    Youth: I will <u>go to church every other Sunday.</u>

RESPONSIBILITY AT HOME AND IN SCHOOL
II. It is my duty and responsibility as a young man to listen and learn at home and in school. Knowledge and Truth are my friends for life.

    Parent-Guardian: I will <u>help you with your homework.</u>

    Youth: I will <u>listen to my teachers and follow instructions.</u>

RELATIONSHIP TO FAMILY, SELF AND COMMUNITY
III. It is my duty and responsibility as a young man to Honor and respect myself, members of my family, and my race.

    Parent-Guardian: I will <u>remind you to say yes ma'am and no ma'am.</u>

    Youth: I will <u>say yes sir and yes ma'am to all adults.</u>

BROTHERHOOD / COMMUNITY / SCHOOL
IV. It is my duty and responsibility to proudly befriend, and stand shoulder to shoulder with the positive young men of my race and the world.

    Parent-Guardian: I will <u>let you play after school every day.</u>

    Youth: I will <u>share my toys and not fight.</u>

Ages 4-11

HONOR MANHOOD RESPONSIBILITIES

V. These four codes I am honor-bound to learn and live. I realize and accept the fact of manhood as a responsibility to myself, my family, and my people.

   Parent-Guardian: I will help you care for your toys and room.

   Youth: I will take care of my toys and room.

   _____

PRIVILEGES AND RESPONSIBILITY

VI. I understand that my privileges are based on my willingness to accept and complete my responsibilities at home and in school.

   Parent-Guardian: I will let you go to the movies and give you an allowance.

   Youth: I will be happy to go to the movies once a week.

   _____

COURAGE, HARD WORK, DIRTY WORK, GOALS

VII. I have courage to face and complete tasks which require hard work, dirty work, and the responsibility to reach my goals and manhood.

   Parent-Guardian: I will help you learn to clean the tub and do dishes.

   Youth: I will learn to clean my tub and do dishes.

   _____

Special agreements or understandings

   I will get a new bike for Christmas if I keep my contract.

   _____

   _____

Youth _____   Date From _____ Date To _____

Parent-Guardian _____   Date From _____ Date To _____

PAAM-U 41

The Code of Honor Family Contract
Ages 12-17

I _____ understand and agree this family contract will govern my behavior attitude and responsibility in the following areas: home, school, community church, and part-time employment. The three C's of Courtesy, Consideration and Cooperation are to be used at all times in all places.

RELIGION / CHURCH / TEMPLE / SPIRITUAL EDUCATION

I. It is my duty and responsibility as a growing man to observe, listen, and study how God works within me, the world, and the universe.

   Parent-Guardian: I will _____

   Youth: I will _____

   _____

RESPONSIBILITY AT HOME AND IN SCHOOL

II. It is my duty and responsibility as a growing man to learn and master positive thought and actions.

   Parent-Guardian: I will _____

   Youth: I will _____

   _____

RELATIONSHIP TO FAMILY, SELF AND COMMUNITY

III. It is my duty and responsibility as a growing man to learn and master our tradition of honoring, respecting, and protecting--our women, children, elderly, and self through love, commitment, guidance, time, and support.

   Parent-Guardian: I will _____

   Youth: I will _____

   _____

BROTHERHOOD / COMMUNITY / SCHOOL

IV. It is my duty and responsibility to proudly befriend and stand shoulder to shoulder with the positive men of my race and the world.

   Parent-Guardian: I will _____

   Youth: I will _____

   _____

Ages 12-17

HONOR MANHOOD RESPONSIBILITIES
V. These four codes I am honor bound to learn and live. I realize and accept the fact of manhood as a responsibility to myself, my family, and my people.

Parent-Guardian: I will _____

Youth: I will _____

_____

PRIVILEGES AND RESPONSIBILITY
VI. I understand that my privileges are based on my willingness to know, except and complete my responsibilities at home and in school.

Parent-Guardian: I will _____

Youth: I will _____

_____

COURAGE, HARD WORK, DIRTY WORK, GOALS
VII. I am courageous, and can face and complete tasks which require hard work, dirty work, and responsibility to reach my goals and manhood.

Parent-Guardian: I will _____

Youth: I will _____

_____

Special agreements or understandings

_____

_____

_____

Youth _____   Date From _____ Date To _____

Parent-Guardian_____   Date From _____ Date To _____

PAAM-U 43

THE TUTORING TRAIN: Point of Light #3

Each One - Teach One

The tutoring train is intended to complement, be an addition to, or replace standard tutoring programs across the nation. Part of the problem we face is that those youth who need tutoring most will not consistently enroll or attend. In the tutoring train philosophy **every child** tutors and is tutored. Each child is tutored by an older child and each child tutors a younger child.

The tutoring responsibility begins at age seven or second grade in consistency with The Code of Honor and Seven Rites of Passage responsibility. The seven year old formally begins to academically tutor children 2-5 years of age. The youth should be given an age appropriate curriculum such as ABCs, numbers 1-10, flash cards, or coloring books as examples. The multiplication tables can only be learned by repetition and coaching by a tutor. The tutoring train diagram using only elementary school grade levels will appear this way.

The 8th grader will tutor the 6th grader.

The 7th grader will tutor the 5th grader.

The 6th grader will tutor the 4th grader.

The 5th grader will tutor the 3rd grader.

The 4th grader will tutor the 2nd grader.

The 3rd grader will tutor the 1st grader.

The 2nd grader will tutor the kindergartner.

The train is intended to continue through high school, college and graduate school. The form of the train may change to specialized classes and tutoring of groups by one tutor. Examples would be freshman and sophomore English in high school and college. Basic mathematics, algebra, geometry, and trigonometry. Individual tutors could rotate turns or sections of material for the same group. High school juniors will tutor high school freshmen in freshmen subject material. High school seniors will tutor high school sophomores. College sophomores will tutor high school seniors and college freshmen will tutor high school juniors. The tutoring train diagram should resemble this:

College seniors will tutor college sophomores.

College juniors will tutor college freshmen.

College sophomores will tutor high school seniors.

College freshmen will tutor high school juniors.

High school seniors will tutor high school sophomores.

High school juniors will tutor high school freshmen.

High school sophomores will tutor junior high 8th graders

High school freshmen will tutor junior high 7th graders.

This same basic formula is to be repeated through graduate and post graduate work. The full cooperation and collaboration of each instructor and school administrator should be enlisted. **The goal is the mastery of all material relevant to a particular course or subject to the best of that student's ability.**

This form of tutoring naturally overlaps into a mentorship relationship for many students. There is also a very important philosophical shift from individual competition for grades to group cooperation, for mastery of information. This shift will bring to the surface special talents and gifts in academic and artistic areas of study. This approach is also in keeping with the PAAM-U philosophy of group cooperation.

Additional benefits of self esteem and self respect will be built. A system of respect for authority and responsibility will be built. Teachers and school systems will have reduced discipline problems, experience fewer drop outs, and be assisted in overloaded classrooms. Fewer African American males will be dumped in special education classifications.

Volunteer tutors can multiply their efforts by supervising 20 youth in pairs of two for 40 minutes. Volunteers can use more creativity and skills related to curriculum. Most important, a tradition of African Americans teaching ourselves will be built, along with respect for each other's knowledge and authority, as early as seven years of age.

Timing

The most ideal setting for the tutoring train is of course in the school setting during school hours. There could be 30 minutes for one group to tutor and 30 minutes for the tutoring group to switch and be tutored. The next choice would be pre-class or after care hours in the school. Other alternatives are after school hours in traditional community centers, church, etc., Saturday school combined with recreation, or food. The choice is up to the individual initiator. The goal is every child tutors and is tutored. Each one-teach one.

MENTORSHIP PROGRAM: Point of Light #4

Each One, Reach One

Definition

The word mentor is of greek origin and myth. The ancient Greeks told of a wise man named Mentor, an advisor to Odysseus and teacher of the hero's son[1]. Mentor means a wise and trusted counselor or teacher, a wise advisor, a trusted guide, tutor, or coach.[2] The two key words in the definition which our programs will focus on are wisdom and trust. The cultural and moral responsibility of guiding the thoughts and actions of an open mind is a great and major responsibility for counselors, teachers, advisors, guides, tutors, coaches and helping professionals.

Basic Mentorship Tools

Mentorship and its meaning are part of all aspects of the Master Plan of Action. The Seven Rites of Passage, Tutoring Train, Conflict Resolution Training, and The Family Contract will offer any mentor more than enough to teach and model. They also offer each youth and mentor a solid foundation for building a personal relationship. Love and positive reinforcement offer the cement to hold each building block in place.

---

[1] Nashville Banner, "Making the most of mentors", November 23, 1992.

[2] Webster Seventh New Collegiate Dictionary, 1971.

Honesty As A Working Tool

A primary ingredient for working with African American youth is honesty. For a mentor to be real and genuine and to be who you really are, is honesty. No person is perfect. We do not recommend you artificially hide your shortcomings and flaws. Let your mentee know through your humanness that they can be positive and successful as they continue to grow, learn and improve themselves. Let them know that no imperfection or shortcoming can limit their desire to go forward. Let them know that acceptance of never ending learning and growth through experience is the foundation of wisdom.

Hypocrisy is the greatest enemy of the generations. Expose your mentee to reality. Every experience does not have to be a picnic, party or entertainment. For example, let your mentee spend a Saturday helping cut grass or doing home repairs. If your normal ritual is to have a beer after you finish your work, don't change or be deceptive for the sake of a super role model image. Have your beer but clarify, this is a privilege for adults and is directly linked to responsibility. It is linked to the lawful responsibility to drink in moderation if you drive; know your limitations so that you do no harm to your loved ones or innocent people; recognize that there is a difference between social drinking and alcoholism; use wisdom and moderation in relationship to any drug which includes nicotine and caffeine.

There is no need to recommend or condemn, each person will have a normal developmental period of experimentation. This type of honesty leads into real conversations concerning the pitfalls of alcohol or chemical dependency that limit a man's ability to fulfill his responsibility and function properly in society. The goal is to teach balance, moderation, and self-discipline, not perfection. You and who you are, the real you, is the best role model. Each mentee will make his own choices as he is confronted with life. Honesty and reality framed in a positive, constructive way is all you can do for your own child or someone else's.

Schools

Mentors are encouraged to attend P.T.A. meetings and be actively involved and communicate with classroom teachers and principles. Teaching professionals who have a reliable resource on the home front feel and relate better to the child's minor infractions.

Team Approach

The team approach to mentorship is a practical and realistic approach. A mentorship team would consist of two to six men. The advantages of the team concept is that it allows flexibility for the natural turnover of mentors due to job, school, family, or health reasons. In the team concept, remaining members step in and replace the lost member until a replacement can be trained or recruited. The team concept also leaves room for rotating work schedule conflicts or the miscellaneous things which prevent us from being in two places at one time.

Programs

Our mentorship programs will include traditional youth activities already in existence: scouting, sports, fraternities, boys clubs, recreation. The framework of activity may differ, but the foundation of the Five Points of Light should have consistency and continuity throughout all activities. Mentorship team input can be integrated into any existing organized activity. For those who want to form new group activities, they can be built around the Five Points of Light. One-to-one mentorship using the team approach will be a standard part of PAAM-U mentorship.

One new element is the Each One Reach One concept. All youth involved in any activity, group or individual, must commit themselves to carrying on this tradition. All youths have an influence on their peers and younger youths.

This influence must be formalized with responsibility for positive leadership. The intent is to create a mushroom effect where youths are not only mentored, but they become mentors at the same time.

Other Considerations

Mentors must be constantly aware of the mentee's family. Your relationship with the youth automatically means a relationship to the family must be built and maintained. We recommend this relationship be friendly, mature, and professional. Testing of boundaries and trust are normal. The best strategy to be used, if ever an uncomfortable situation arises, is tact and refocusing the relationship on what is in the best interest of the child. Confidentiality and respect for the family is maintained at all times.

Adult Mentorship

Every African American adult has a responsibility to mentor someone younger or below them in experience or status. Each African American adult has the responsibility to accept mentorship from a person older, wiser, more experienced, and/or above them in status. ALL PAAM-U persons are required to show respect, and honor their seniors.

CONFLICT RESOLUTION, MEDIATION, ORGANIZATION AND LEADERSHIP TRAINING: Point of Light #5

We define Conflict Resolution as the peaceful non-violent settlement of differences or disputes between two or more people, groups or organizations settled by those parties. We define mediation as a peaceful non-violent settlement of differences or disputes with a mutually agreed upon neutral party listening to all sides and helping to find a satisfactory agreement.

Conflict Resolution and Mediation will explore every avenue available and known to human beings to settle disputes and differences without violence, fairly and justly. This will include but not be limited to individuals, families and groups.

The primary focus will be elementary school systems, public housing, and families. The primary training will be in the progress and skills for conflict resolution and mediation. Related topics which are included in this training are:

- Understanding Conflicts
- Non-Violent Communication Skills
- Intergroup Relations
- Multicultural Education
- Community Building
- Power
- Disappointment
- Rejection
- Anger
- Assertiveness

The Codes of Honor and Five Points of Light give a solid foundation for teaching conflict resolution and mediation. This advantage of a value base gives an added working tool to peacefully resolve differences when all elements of sincerity are present. Each course needs to be tailored by the community and participants of PAAM-U for their specific needs.

Organization and Leadership

Organization and leadership training are a must for any progressive movement. We will present each model of organizational structure and business for our participants. The goal is to be able to organize, meet, set goals, complete goals, and move to each new objective efficiently, in a timely manner, and on time. Meetings which last from one hour to one hour and a half and which start and end on time will benefit all parties. One goal that will be helpful is to establish a separate time period for those who wish to ventilate their frustration or talk without a point.

The <u>preparation and training</u> of all parties to learn to be good leaders and good workers are essential. As we cross areas in our basket weave of coverage, one way may be a leader in a given area but come under the leadership of someone else as they cross areas.

Wisdom-Teaching Of Our Elders:

*It is wise to discuss problems,
only in the framework of solutions.*

THE TEN PLACES FOR ACTION

The ten places for action are ten areas of our society which represent the greatest opportunity for fulfilling the duty and responsibility we have to establish our culture. These areas represent a criss-cross and basket weave of overlapping care and contact which forms a cultural basket to protect 95% of our people.

The following ten areas and explanations represent the initial outline of what can be built using the Code of Honor and Five Points of Light. With each of these ten areas, an administrative planning and management component must be included. Efficient, well planned organizations with no time wasted will be our greatest asset in keeping volunteers and affiliates working.

The Ten Places of Action are:

1. **The Family**
2. **Our Elders**
3. **Religious institutions and organizations**
4. **Health care and educational systems**
5. **Correctional systems/Chemical Dependency**
6. **Helping professions, business, science, art**
7. **Veterans, unions, fraternities, sororities, social clubs**
8. **Community, community centers, sports, recreation**
9. **African American Recognition and Unity Month**
   (Black History Month renamed and Rededicated)
10. **The African American National Institute of Achievement and Culture**

THE FAMILY: Action Area #1

Pre-Conception Prayer and Pre-Natal Care

We define family as those people with whom you are related through love or blood line. Our first action goal is to promote and establish unity among African American people around the values and actions needed for spiritual, mental, emotional, physical, health, and development for all.

The family is the foundation of our culture and race. Historically, the African American family has been the victim or beneficiary of political and economic change. It has only been one hundred years since our total population has had the legal right to marry. As victims of oppression it is unrealistic to expect our family units to perfectly mirror the dominant culture. Love, positive reinforcement, communication, patience, flexibility, and understanding are the best working tools any family can use. No matter how strong or weak parents' interpersonal relationships are, our children must be the number one priority. The greatest injustice we can do as parents is to use our children as weapons against each other. Please declare a truce around children's issues as you struggle for individual needs. Each child wants to love their mom and dad the same. To take away something positive or project something negative to a child about his father or mother takes a piece of the child with it.

We Are All Family

For years there has been the idea that a parent is only responsible for their own children. There is no escape or safe place of isolation in America. No matter how carefully you watch or teach, sooner or later you will be touched by the overall condition of our people. The child you ignore may be the child your child brings home or parents a child with your child.

Healthy Babies - Action Goal # 1

The primary enemies of healthy babies are:

1. The infant mortality rate of African American babies
2. The low birth weight of babies
3. Lack of pre-natal care
4. Lack of infant care for the first year. When the child's brain grows to 2/3 of its final size.

The facts and figures for the condition of our babies are poor. The research will fill volumes. One article which states our situation clearly and briefly is from The Wall Street Journal, June 4, 1992, B-1 by Ron Winslow. In this article they stated:

1. Infants born to college educated black parents are nearly twice as likely to die within a year as those born to college educated white couples.

2. Researchers state the higher mortality rate among babies results almost entirely from low birth weights under 5.5 pounds.

3. The current gap of 17.2 deaths per 1,000 live births among African Americans compared to 8.2 deaths for whites represents the difference.

4. Researchers have generally attributed the difference in black and white infant mortality rates to poverty, restricted access to medical care and other socioeconomic tables that plague African Americans. But now researchers have revealed no matter what indicators you look at African American infants are more likely to die than white infants, college educated parents included.

The Plan

The plan is simple education and action, incorporating the need for pre-conception prayer and prenatal care in our culture. When our children begin to play with dolls and pretend families is when we begin to educate. Story books, video tapes, and parent curricula taught over and over until it is as much a part of our children as their music, clothes, and television. The lessons will begin with stories like this: **Mary prayed for a healthy baby after she and Ken were married. She ate good healthy meals and stayed away from unhealthy things. Before she had her baby she saw the doctor from the beginning to the end. She took vitamins, ate well and exercised. One day, "walah," she had a fat healthy baby boy (or girl) that looked just like she thought it would. After the baby was born she took him to the baby doctor for check ups all the time and fed him good healthy food until he was one year old and ready for his first hair cut.**

Stories like this are not threatening or difficult for parents yet they teach important values of a spiritual connection and prayer around the conception of our children and good pre-natal and infant care. There is nothing wrong with praying to have children who will be a credit to themselves and the world. If you ask it shall be given. If you ask for nothing how can you receive anything. If you believe your child is a blessing from God, regardless of the timing, and treat that child as a blessing from God, teach that child that they are a blessing from God with a contribution to offer to the world, your child will be a blessing and will make a contribution. By teaching our children to pray for healthy babies who contribute to the world, we receive healthy babies who contribute to the world.

This one example can be represented in thousands of different ways. As our people unite and our talented and professional people merge, standard stories, lessons, and curricula will emerge.

Notes

1. Stages of development: parents and children should be familiar with goals and tasks of each developmental stage. Pride teams will study and teach developmental stages.

2. Interpersonal relationships and cross sexual communication will be explored and taught in the context of a people under attack from within and without.

3. Each family member will have a home record which includes a complete medical and dental history and a complete educational record with goals. This record is to be updated upon each change or new occurrence.

4. Alternative forms of discipline will be studied and taught.

"Pride" Parents Small Group or Team

The word **pride** has a meaning in addition to how a person may feel about themselves, someone or something. **Pride** is a term used to describe the African lion's family unit. We have adopted this term to describe our small parent groups or teams because of the dual meaning of the word.

We encourage single parents, married couples, and couples living together to form small groups for the purpose of having and raising healthy well rounded and disciplined children. No parent or prospective parent should be without a **pride** for information, reinforcement and support.

Prides also help our mentorship teams to narrow their efforts by meeting with groups who are organized and know what their needs are. These groups should be formed with people who have a common interest and relate well to each other. They should be open to receive new families in transition and assist them in finding compatible **prides**. They should also be active educational and teaching units for new **prides**. The recommended number in each **pride** is no more than 20 persons counting all household members.

Memorial Prides

Memorial prides will consist of parents and family of those youth who have died as victims of oppression. Any child who died of reasons other than natural causes is eligible for nomination for a memorial membership and their family entitled to appropriate affiliation under that membership.

PAAM-U is committed to ensure the children who have died as a result of street violence, drugs, in prison or of AIDS will be remembered forever and their deaths will not be in vain. This **prides** work will be centered on eliminating the needless deaths of our children. **Until we are willing to honor our dead we cannot care for our living**.

African American Recognition and Unity Month

The **memorial prides** and their lost loved ones will be recognized and honored by memorial services during youth week. Youth week is the third week in February. The planning and coordination of these services should be managed by **memorial prides**.

Memorial Wing
The African American National Institute of Achievement and Culture

A wing of the African American National Institute of Achievement and Culture will be dedicated to the memory of our lost children. A picture and biography of each child lost to unnatural causes which relate to our condition are planned to be in place in this wing.

OUR ELDERS: Action Area #2

The relationship between the young and old is a primary part of The Master Plan of Action. This relationship places all adults with responsibility to those older than themselves and those younger than themselves. In theory, there will always be someone who is older and elder to you, and someone who is younger, that you are elder to.

Every adult African American man and woman is an elder and steward to our race and culture. We are responsible to God to plan for the safety, care and protection of our most vulnerable persons. Both the terms elder and elderly will be used in reference to our senior citizens and this action area. Elder will be used more to refer to status and elderly used more to refer to conditions of greater dependency.

The elderly and our responsibility to them is probably our simplest and most direct action area. It is our duty to honor, respect, and protect our elderly. Elders will fulfill this duty by forming peace patrol teams in every community. These elders will have the power and authority to draft any African American man or youth into on-the-spot, temporary service for the purpose of helping an elderly person.

Peace Patrol

The peace patrol will focus on four basic areas:

1. Transportation
2. Security, home, and community
3. Advocacy--short and long term
4. Yearly health and benefit chart

Every elderly or disabled person will be listed and accounted for. The peace patrol teams will include affiliates, volunteers, and the elderly themselves as primary advisors.

The primary functions will be to organize a structured transportation and security system that ensures our elderly travel to and from their destinations safely. Each elderly person should have a standard yearly chart which lists regular medical appointments and renewal dates on benefits, pharmacists, doctors, and contact persons to call for concerns. We will have active persons who lobby and work for improved services for the concerns and problems of our elderly. We must also network with existing organizations who share our goals.

African American Recognition and Unity Month

During the first week in February, **Wisdom Week**, our elders and wise should be honored in the churches, temples, and community centers across the nation. Our peace patrols will have primary responsibility for the planning and coordination of this week.

Cultural Wisdom Wing

The African American National Institute of Achievement and Culture

A wing of this institute will be dedicated to the wisdom-teaching of our elders from Africa through slavery and present times. The intent is that the wisdom of the past create a foundation of present and future progress. There is a need to know what works, what does not work, and under what conditions the two vary. Writing, photography, audio tape, video tape, and film will be used to package this information for educational and motivational tools to include all age groups.

RELIGIOUS INSTITUTIONS AND ORGANIZATIONS:
Action Area #3

The challenge of African American religious institutions and organizations being united through a common positive cultural value is fantastic. Even as we agree to disagree on our particular faith, we can agree to agree on our future generations survival. If there are no African American people there will be no African American church. If the present rate of self destruction continues, by the year 2,000, 70% of our young men under 25 will be in jail or under court supervision. After God, we are all we have left. Before we can convert any person we must get them in church, and before we can do that they must be living and breathing. PAAM-U assists religious institutions by cultivating our culture. We affirm a foundation of God, family, and spiritual responsibility, which supports all churches.

It is the duty of all serious and committed religious leaders and organizations to unite our people in establishing a cultural foundation for meaningful religion to flourish. All members of all religious organizations should clarify and vigorously adopt **The One Code of Honor** as their cultural base for manhood. Not only will **The One Code of Honor for Men** bring men back to the church, but it will give a foundation for all religious teaching.

African America Recognition and Unity Month (AARUM)

Local religious institutions and organizations will be responsible for hosting AARUM services, celebration and festivities. Ministers across the nation can add the four topics of wisdom of the elders, our women our children, and our men to Sunday services, Wednesday meetings, and special activities for the month.

African American Unity Prayer

The unity prayer should begin and end each gathering and service.

Seven Rites of Passage

Ministers and religious leaders are encouraged to be on call to initiate the first Rite of Passage at the birth of each child. Formal Rites of Passage Ceremonies for all male members of your organization can be done in unison each year.

Family Contract: Conflict Resolution

Ministers and religious leaders can facilitate the family contract and conflict resolution and act as mediators between opposing parties.

Tutoring and Mentorship

Each religious facility should have a tutoring train and mentorship program.

Mentorship

As each institution and organization reaches out to incorporate more lives under its protective wings, each will grow and prosper in its turn. Affiliates from within your organization are expected to form teams to facilitate The Master Plan. Ministers should not be saddled with additional responsibilities of organization or implementation.

Religious Wing - The African American National Institute of Achievement and Culture

A wing of this institute will be dedicated to past and present religions of African and African American peoples. We intend to recognize each denomination and the significant founders, present day leaders, and aspiring future leaders. Writing, photography, video tapes and film will be used to package this information for educational and motivational tools to include all age groups.

HEALTH CARE SYSTEMS AND EDUCATIONAL SYSTEMS:
Action Area #4

Health Care Systems include all public and private facilities or practices which serve African American people and all African American persons working or volunteering in any capacity within the health care (public or private) industry.

The goal is to have complete knowledge and involvement of all African Americans in the health industry. This involvement should be both personal and professional. Each health care provider is a cornerstone of our race and culture. Health issues begin with prenatal care and continue through geriatrics. Our common enemies are ignorance, indifference, oppression, poverty and disunity.

Positive African American Men-United provides a vehicle for networking services which will improve the health standards of our race and fulfill the priorities of our health care professionals.

African American health care providers and educators shall:

1. Affiliate themselves with PAAM-U.
2. Commit themselves to the Code of Honor and Master Plan of Action.
3. Affiliate their professional organizations as part of our national network.
4. Volunteer time for needed services, training, and education in the community.
5. Work with health teams and education teams.

Health Care Teams

We will form Health Care Teams composed of professionals, paraprofessionals, volunteers, and parents. These teams will be responsible for insuring every African American has a home health record and plan. They will also be responsible for having at least one PAAM-U representative or liaison person in place during operational hours for all prenatal facilities, maternity wards, pediatric, and geriatric facilities. The overall purpose is to insure we have a basket weave of overlapping communication and contact to cover every African American as they enter or leave the world.

Prenatal liaisons: will at least inform each expectant mother and father of PAAM-U, check on diet needs, and pre-arrange the first rite of passage for after delivery.

Maternity ward liaisons: will communicate and comfort parents and relatives, be responsible for the first rite of passage at birth, if possible, and follow up to a pediatric liaison referral and meetings.

Pediatric liaisons: will take referrals from maternity and insure each child has a home health record, medical, and nutritional needs met during the first year of infancy. They will make referrals to the next appropriate liaison and the community team.

Geriatric liaisons: will insure that all elderly citizens have responsible relatives or guardians to insure their health and well being on a personal level.

Health Care Wing

The African American National Institute of Achievement and Culture

A wing of this institute will be dedicated to past, present, and future development of health care achievements and contributions. The history of African American involvement and contributions in the areas of science, research, and practice will be accurately reflected in writing, photography, video, and film presentations. These presentations will be used as educational and motivational tools to include all age groups.

Educational Systems

We define educational systems as all facilities that serve to teach African American people, from day care and private baby sitters to university graduate schools. This definition is also to include the home, community, religious institution, and job. All areas are responsible for actively participating in The Codes of Honor and Master Plan of Action. The tutoring train and mentorship programs should be in place in all educational systems serving African American people.

Educational Priorities

PAAM-U is setting educational priorities based on our greatest need for the future. With the following solid foundation each person can go on to choose their individual areas of concentration:

1. Mathematics
2. Science
3. History
4. Languages

We Will Reclaim Our Children and Schools

The battle of parent against teacher, against principle, against school board will end. We will agree to work together for the betterment of each child and the focus will be on what is best for the child. Parents must be contained and trained in positive communication techniques. We are going to establish an atmosphere where every responsible adult has the freedom and authority to teach and correct any child. We will encourage on the spot correction that is supported by secondary correction in the home, by the parent.

Rule #1: Inform the parent of any misbehaving of any child.

Rule #2: Be happy and appreciative to anyone who informs you about your child's misbehavior.

Rule #3: Parents talk to each other on the phone and face to face, never losing sight of your common goal, your child.

Educational Teams

We will form educational teams composed of professionals, paraprofessional volunteers and parents. These teams will be responsible for having in place at least one liaison person, one advocate, one social worker, and community worker for complete cross communication concerning any African American's child and his or her academic, social, and behavioral progress. This team is there for the purpose of increasing positive communication and education. To encourage appropriate techniques which include, rather than exclude, our energetic and creative youth. They are responsible for plans which keep a balance of self-esteem, learning and discipline. Overburdened public institutions must feel they have support, and that no problem child is without a caring adult to assist teachers and administrators.

These teams will also be responsible for development and implementation of alternative programs which meet the needs of the students they serve. From the tutoring train to Saturday schools, every possible alternative which makes learning fun, exciting, and relevant should be explored. Each child should have educational goals and a plan in their home file, education section. Educational teams should cover:

A. Day Care
B. Pre School
C. Kindergarten
D. Elementary Schools
E. Junior High Schools
F. High Schools
G. Colleges and Universities
H. Graduate Schools

Learning and Education Wing

The African American National Institute of Achievement and Culture

The institute will dedicate a wing to the history, present achievement and future research and development of learning and education system. We will also recognize African American educators and learning researchers. Standardization of successful approaches to learning and discipline will also be promoted. The concepts of schools without failure and total participation schools for activities will also be presented. Writing, photography, audio tape, video tape, and film will be used to package this information for educational and motivational tools to include all age groups.

CORRECTIONAL SYSTEMS/CHEMICAL DEPENDENCY: Action Area #5

A Triple Tragedy

It is a tragedy that 23% of our young men between the ages of 20-29 are under the control of the criminal justice system[3]--in prison or jail, on probation or parole. At the current rate of growth this figure will have increased to 70% of our male population under 29, by the year 2000, 100% by the year 2005.

It is a double tragedy that 95% of our people who have been incarcerated, needed to be in jail to protect the public and the offenders from themselves.

It is a triple tragedy that the majority of our convicted felons will reenter society with no more skills, money, motivation, or consciousness than when they entered the correctional system.

The figures vary on chemical dependency but it is fairly safe to say the majority of our convicted felons were under the influence of drugs or alcohol when arrested.

Pros and Cons

The problems we face in dealing with this population is that inexperienced volunteers are of no value. The only people qualified to work with this segment of our brothers and sisters are those who have come from the experience or those who have been professionally trained and have meaningful work experiences.

The goal is to implement the Code of Honor and Master Plan of Action within the AA/NA (Alcoholics Anonymous/Narcotics Anonymous), co-dependent groups behind the

---

[3] Based on Figures from the United States Justice Department and The Sentencing Project

walls and in the Free World. All positive growth groups with African Americans' participation should be networked. Teams of professionals and convicts or pros and cons can work together to create a cultural foundation which inspires hope and give objective definitions and frameworks. For those who have given up hope for themselves, this program offers a preventive tool for their loved ones. From behind prison walls a man may give to his son those values and training which keep him from following his father's foot steps. The expectation is that each generation will do better and be more than the last. It is not where you come from that matters but where you are going and how you plan to get there. The reality, that our greatest minds and future pool of African American genius has been systematically channeled to correctional systems, must be faced.

Against All Odds Wing

The African American National Institute of Achievement and Culture

We will dedicate a wing of the institute to the pitfalls of man and to those who have successfully overcome those pitfalls. Writing, audio tape, video tape, and film will be used to package this information for educational and motivational tools to include all age groups.

HELPING PROFESSIONALS, BUSINESSES, SCIENCE, AND ART: Action Area #6

These areas represent a common bond and interest that relates directly to the human condition. African Americans who work or have interest in these areas should network to.

1. Develop yourself personally.
2. To develop your family and loved ones.
3. To develop the African American peoples and communities you serve.
4. To use your influence for unity and consciousness.

These categories cover all aspects of the medical field, helping professions, science and arts, including the performing arts. Business includes all aspects of business from accounting to sales.

Teams should be formed under local chapters to assist in any way needed. This area has the greatest resources to generate needed funds and publicity in your industrial areas.

Prerequisite for Internship

The Code of Honor and Master Plan should be a prerequisite of those you intern or mentor. That which you have achieved should go to those who are committed to assist our people and the unity of our people. The assistance on all other areas of action is needed but a team approach of professionals united is also needed.

The African American National Institute of Achievement and Culture

The institute will have wings for the helping professions, business, science, art, and performing arts. African American Achievements and Contributions will be recorded past, present, and future development. Writing, audio tape, video tape, film, and theater will be used to package this information for educational and motivational tools, to include all ages.

VETERANS, UNIONS, FRATERNITIES, SORORITIES, AND SOCIAL CLUBS: Action Area #7

Veterans, unions, fraternities, sororities, and social clubs can, by your nature, understand the value and power of unity. African Americans who are members of the above mentioned groups are asked to form teams within your group for:

1. **Personal and family development**
2. **Leadership and full participation of African American Recognition and Unity Month Activities**
3. **To establish PAAM-U commitment as a requirement for membership in your organization**
4. **To network community work and efforts through PAAM-U.**

The setting of priorities is important to the commitment to any union, fraternity, sorority, or social club and must be based on a greater commitment to your race and culture. Active involvement in The Five Points of Light will yield benefits to all families.

The African American National Institute of Achievements and Culture

A wing of the institute will be dedicated to the history and contribution of African Americans in unions, fraternities, sororities, and social clubs. A separate wing will be established for veterans and the history of our people in the military. Writing, audio tape, video tape, and film will be used to package this information for educational and motivational purposes including all age groups.

COMMUNITY, COMMUNITY CENTERS, SPORTS, AND RECREATION: Action Area #8

This area is one of our most challenging and also represents potential for our greatest grass roots involvement.

Community Teams

Each community, depending on its population and density, should have at least <u>one</u> community leadership team for every 100 people or for every 10 square blocks. This team should be composed of no less than 5 people. This team should know, by first and last name, every person, man, woman and child in their area. Unit by unit (house, apartment, or room) floor by floor, street by street. This team is responsible for the total and overall welfare of that population.

The community leadership team should represent a cross section of that community: men, women, youth, professionals, and street wise persons. Teams should work closely with other teams that border their areas to form communication and working networks. Each team should have working relationships with schools, health care centers, helping professionals, business, and recreational centers that service their district. The team will handle specific problems of family communication of their people and refer other problems to the appropriate action areas in the Master Plan. This team will assist in the establishment of Prides, monitor the Rites of Passage, Family Contracts, Tutoring Trains, and Mentorship programs.

They insure each child has a home file which contains at least a health plan and an educational plan.

A national grid will be drawn to cover every square foot of America and every African American. The community team is the center of all activity. They should operate and meet at local community recreational centers. They are responsible for organizing and recruiting community advisory boards. They have the option of:

1. Using existing community boards.
2. Recruiting representatives from existing community boards who represent the concerns of the existing board.
3. Forming new advisory boards.

The community leadership team is to have major involvement and participation with and on the PAAM-U Executive Committee.

Sports and Recreation

All persons connected with community centers will benefit from <u>full</u> membership and participation with PAAM-U. This is to include community center personnel, coaches, trainers, referees, umpires, officials, and their supervisors. The Code of Honor and Master Plan give all of the above a powerful and valuable tool in working with our children and youth. Community centers, sports and recreation workers can concentrate on their own particular task while having resources to deal with any problem or concern readily available and accessible.

Professional, College, and Developing Athletes

Professional, collegiate, and developing athletes have a united network and vehicle in place to interact with grass roots community people. Speaking engagements, clinics, and personal talks with family prides can be arranged quickly, efficiently, and quietly.

The African American National Institute of Achievement and Culture

Individual wings will be dedicated to African American achievements and contributions to sports, recreation, and entertainment in their past, present, and future development. Writing, audio tape, video tape, film, and performing arts will be used to package this information for educational and motivational programs including all age groups.

AFRICAN AMERICAN RECOGNITION AND UNITY MONTH (AARUM): Action Area #9

Black History Month Renamed and Rededicated
February 1st - 28th (29th)

1 *Week Number* *Week Name* *February*	I Wisdom Week 1st - 7th	II Women's Week 8th - 14th	III Youth Week 15th - 21st	IV Men's Week 22nd - 28th
2 Population Recognized and Honored	The Wise Our Elders The Disabled	Young Women 4-11 yrs old, Teen Women 12-17 yrs old, Women 18 yrs and over	Infants Babies Children Youth Teens	Young Men 4-11 yrs old, Teen Men 12-17 yrs old, Men 18 yrs and over
3 Duty	HONOR (Respect) (Protect) UNITY	RESPECT (Protect) (Honor) UNITY	PROTECT (Honor) (Respect) UNITY	UNITY Honor Respect Protect
4 Time Period	Past and History	Present Conditions	Future Improvement	Challenges Past, Present, Future
5 Positive Goals from activities of the week and month	Wisdom Consciousness Humility from our history Changing anger to constructive actions	Co-operation Balancing life and feelings	Talent Development Setting Goals Faith in God and life	Unity Duty honor responsibility over pride and ego for generations to come

Why Rename Black History Month

The recognition of Carter G. Woodson and his creation of Black History month and its contribution cannot be measured. The renaming of Black History month is dedicated to Carter G. Woodson. It is with the greatest admiration for Mr. Woodson that we seek to improve and make more meaningful the month of February.

The renaming of Black History month to African American Recognition and Unity Month allows our people an opportunity to become more specific at recognizing the achievements, contributions, and value of our four specific groups: elders, women, children, and men. While we examine the history and present condition, we can plan strategies for the improving future. During African American Recognition and Unity Month, every aspect of our people can be reviewed and dedicated to the unity and progress of our people. (See Table)

1. The Four Weeks

The month has been divided into four natural seven day weeks and named in honor of a specific group of our population:

I.   Wisdom Week
II. Woman's Week
III. Youth Week
IV. Men's Week

2. The Population

The four populations represented in the four weeks are:

I.   Wisdom Week - The Wise, Our Elders, The Disabled
II. Women's Week - Young Women, Teen Women, Adult Women
III. Youth Week - Infants, Babies, Children, Youth, Teens
IV. Men's Week - Young Men, Teen Men, Adult Men

3. Duty

In number "3" a particular duty is emphasized in each of the four weeks. This duty represents men's responsibility to that population. It also represents the race's duty and that population's duty to itself.

All four duties are applicable to all four populations but the emphasis placed on one particular aspect allows us an opportunity to focus:

I. Honor - Elders
II. Respect - Women
III. Protect - Children
IV. Unity - Man's Duty

4. Era

In the era we can focus on a specific time period for study and emphasis with the idea of future improvement:

I. Past: The honoring of our wise and elders and looking at the past contributions of our ancestors from Africa through slavery has important lessons and should produce wisdom within the culture.

II. Present: The study of women's issues and contributions from slavery to present day is intended to lead us to a goal emphasized in number "5".

III. Future: The week of looking at children's issues to see what can be done and what has worked, when and where.

IV. Unity: The principle of unity week applies to past, present, and future challenges.

5. Positive Goal

In Number "5" we seek to add meaning and purpose to each week with a beginning place for learning, growth and improvement.

AFRICAN AMERICAN RECOGNITION AND UNITY MONTH (AARUM)

Activities Outline

I. WISDOM WEEK

1. Review of African American History
2. Recognition of Our Elders - The oldest people in your community
3. Recognition of the **Peace Patrol**
4. Objective Gift Giving

II. WOMEN'S WEEK

1. Principles of Womanhood
2. 10 Short and Long Term Goals
3. Review of African American Women's History and Issues
4. Objective Gift Giving

III. YOUTH WEEK

1. Truce Day (no youth violence of any kind on this day)
2. 10 Short and Long Term Goals
3. Review of Youth Issues - History, Present, and Future
4. Objective Gift Giving
5. Memorial Services/By Memorial Prides

IV. MEN'S WEEK

1. Code of Honor Ceremony for All Males
2. Sunday United Services. National Hook-up
3. 10 Short and Long Term Goals
4. Objective Gift Giving

THE AFRICAN AMERICAN NATIONAL INSTITUTE OF ACHIEVEMENT AND CULTURE: Action Area #10

The African American National Institute of Achievement and Culture will be located in the Washington, D.C. area. It is time that African Americans have a central institute in our nation's capital which accurately reflects our complete contributions to the United States and the world. This institute will have the complete records and data of every African American achievement and contribution--past, present, and future from A-Z.

State of the Art Communication and Production Center

It is intended that this institute also serve as a state of the art communication and production center, with a dual center located in the Los Angeles area. These centers will include television, radio and stage facilities, with video, audio, and photographic reproduction capacity.

Education and Mentorship Tools

The production of video-taped biographies, autobiographies, and career information tapes on every field of endeavor African Americans have, or hope to participate in, from A-Z, is our goal. Tapes will be made available for loan or purchase to the general public.

The General Public

The museum which will house the contributions and cultural aspects of our history will be open to the general public. The National Institute will have a separate building fund and endowment fund for its construction and continuation.

V

ORGANIZATIONAL

INFORMATION

Positive African American Men-United, Incorporated is the formal organization created as a vehicle for those who desire to fully participate in the Cultural Revolution and Progress of African American People.

Formal affiliation is not required for individual use of the principles and values in this book.

ORGANIZATIONAL INFORMATION
POSITIVE AFRICAN AMERICAN MEN-UNITED, INC.

Classification

Positive African American Men-United, Inc. is a chartered nonprofit network organization for the cultural enrichment of African American people.

Purpose

The purpose of PAAM-U, Inc. is to unite all positive African American men around an objective definition of manhood, based on the relationship to, and the values of, God (Higher Power), positive thought and action, race integrity, family, and brotherhood. Further, that this objective definition of African American manhood and value system be placed within the framework of a Code Of Honor and Pledge to be pursued, lived out, and passed from generation to generation, for the purpose of adding peace, prosperity, honor, and integrity to our race and all of humanity.

Mission

1. To raise generations of children who are healthy, polite, well mannered and reflect home training in their attitude and behavior.

2. To develop our children into positive men and women who honorably contribute to themselves and the world.

3. To encourage, train and support our positive men and women to relate and interact with each other as ladies and gentlemen.

Goals

1. To promote and establish unity among African American people around the values and actions needed for spiritual, mental, emotional, and physical health and development of all.

2. To promote and establish The One Code of Honor for Men as the national standard for African American manhood and The Master Plan of Action as the unifying vehicle for the development of all.

3. To promote and establish national professional standard methods of recruitment, training, education, communication, and evaluation of our staff, volunteers, and beneficiaries.

4. To promote and establish Positive African American Men-United, Inc. as the national unifying network and umbrella resource center for existing organizations or those who wish to form new organizations.

5. To promote and establish a national state of the art, data bank research facility and communication system for African American people and programs.

6. To promote and establish **The African American National Institute of Achievement and Culture**. This institution is to accurately reflect African American history, culture, group, and individual achievements from A-Z-past, present, and future.

7. To promote and establish the use of this organization's ideas and visions as a cultural offensive with no direct political or religious affiliations or ties.

8. To promote and establish the primary focus of African American progress in the first seven years of each child's life, beginning with the first Rite of Passage at birth.

Policy of Unity Above Politics and Religion

In the spirit and name of unity, this organization encourages and supports each person's religious faith and political persuasion regardless of classification. We consider the diversity of African Americans in politics and religion as positive, pragmatic, and beneficial to our race and culture. In that same spirit and name of unity this organization must refrain from ever promoting or endorsing any one particular political party, candidate, religious affiliation, denomination, or leader over another. Within the framework of our organizations and programs, all differences are secondary to our unity in accomplishing the purpose and goals of PAAM-U.

Honor System

PAAM-U, Inc. will be organized and administered on the Honor System. It is the responsibility of each person to honor, respect, and protect this organization, its purpose and goals, from any internal or external threat. Each person is honor-bound to act with honesty and integrity doing the best that can be done in all areas and to be judged by themselves and God. Those who find their way into our ranks who, for any reason, threaten our unity should be sanctioned with compassion and offered help for their particular problem. The local Executive Committee is in charge of all Code of Honor violations and misconduct. Those individuals who, for whatever reason, from mental or emotional imbalance, to purposeful dishonesty, who need to be eliminated from any participation should be reported to the national organization.

Member, Participant, Supporter, Patron

Affiliation with PAAM-U is divided into four basic classifications: member, participant, supporter, and patron. The following is an explanation of each classification:

I. <u>Member</u>: This classification is for African American men and teen men who are fully committed to PAAM-U, its Code of Honor, purpose, goals, philosophy and programs.

<u>Memorial Member</u>: This classification is for either surviving parents of a child whose life was lost to the oppressive conditions under which our people exist. Examples would be street violence, drive-by-shootings, drug overdose, death in prison, murder, or suicide. The surviving parents are awarded a memorial membership in that child's name and are to be honored in February, during African American recognition and unity month, for this supreme sacrifice.

II. <u>Participant</u>: This classification is for African American women and teen women who are fully committed to PAAM-U, its Code of Honor, purpose, goals, philosophy, and programs.

III. <u>Supporter</u>: This classification is for African Americans and non-African Americans who wish to officially contribute to, support, or participate in PAAM-U, its training or programs.

IV. <u>Patrons</u>: Groups, organizations, institutions or businesses that wish to contribute to, support or participate in PAAM-U, its training or programs.

Dues and Registration Costs

DUES		COST
1.	Member	$50.00
2.	Participant	$50.00
3.	Students	$25.00
4.	Elders (over 65)	No Cost
5.	Memorial Member	No Cost

REGISTRATION		
1.	Supporter	$50.00
2.	Patron	$100.00

Dues and registration costs are due July 1st of each year. Member, participant, and student dues may also be paid semi-annually or quarterly. Member, participant, and supporter costs of $50.00 a year equal approximately $.97 per week.

Coverage

I. <u>Member</u>:

    A. Each member and their household, with the exception of males over 18 years of age.

    B. Outside of household, children and their mothers or guardians with the exception of males over 18 years of age.

Each family member's affiliation is to be established at the most appropriate level.

II. <u>Participant</u>:

    A. Each participant and their household with the exception of males over 18.

    B. Outside of household children and their guardians with the exception of males over 18 years of age.

III. <u>Supporter</u>:

Official registration as a PAAM-U supporter covers the individual only.

IV. <u>Patron</u>:

Official registration as a patron covers that specific group, organization, institution or business, entity or branch only.

Affiliation Requirement

Everyone is required to contribute a minimum of 1-4 hours a week public service worker or self improvement time. (This can be arranged on a monthly or quarterly basis.)

What You Can Do: Local and Community Level

PAAM-U will provide a volunteer(s) to act as workers or liaisons in every public and private facility and institution that serves African American people in the United States of America. The purpose is to monitor and establish a rapport and basket weave of contact, to ensure full services and work toward future improvement.

Power and Control - Executive Committee/Advisory Board

Control will rest with the Advisory Board. The Advisory Board will make recommendations to the Executive Committee based on the needs, problems, success, and failure in that particular community, city, or state. The Advisory Board is composed of concerned positive citizens who support PAAM-U's purpose, goals, and philosophy. They report to the Executive Committee the questions, concerns, and problems they see in the community. No new boards have to be formed. For example, existing public housing community boards can be incorporated in the PAAM-U umbrella with no name change, with the gain of a unified national information and advisory network behind them. Communities may choose to pool members from a variety of existing board to form a PAAM-U board.

The Executive Committee is composed of PAAM-U men and youth. They have the responsibility of internal organizational requirements and providing answers and solutions to the questions and problems of the community as seen by the Advisory Board.

The recommended working size for the community Advisory Board is 7-11 members. The recommended size for PAAM-U Executive Committee is 5-7 members.

The limitations of the board and committee are in its interpretations of those areas which are internal to our culture and which we have control over, through our own effort, as opposed to those things which are external and are part of the system of oppression.

      Example: Unemployment - external

                        School Dropouts - internal

One prevailing issue must be kept in mind by the Board and Executive Committee. We do not intend to duplicate or compete with that already in existence. We intend to fill the void that exists in our culture that has the effect of weakening the positive organizations already in existence. We don't need two NAACPs, Urban Leagues, or PUSH. All questions or problems that fall directly under the jurisdiction, control, or expertise of existing African American organizations will be referred to them. PAAM-U will fully support these organization with whatever is needed to provide an impact for positive progressive improvement.

Outline Flow of Concerns: Executive Committees and Advisory Boards

1) Community	3) County	5) State	7) National
2) City	4) State/Region	6) National/Region	

Funding

Where PAAM-U gets its money will determine to a large extent who it is accountable to and what the organization is as a whole. The undertaking of uniting our race must be funded by positive African American people and our true supporters in order to maintain our identity and integrity. The goals and objectives of PAAM-U must remain intact and beyond any manipulation through monetary control. History and statistics prove African Americans have the power and money to do anything positive they pursue in unity.

The time line for this first phase is twenty one years (21 years). By the end of this first phase, we pray to see at least one generation of young men become positive, strong, and united.

Division of Dues

Local Chapter	50%	National Institute	12.5%
National Chapter	25%	Endowment Fund	12.5%

Contributions and Designated Gifts
All gifts and contributions unless designated for a special purpose or fund will be divided by the above formula exactly as dues.

Contributors have the option of designating gifts and contributions to any specific area of PAAM-U, Inc. 12.5% of any designated gift will go to the endowment fund and 87.5% will go directly to the designated area or fund.

Separate accounts will be maintained for, The National Organization, The African American National Institute for Achievement and Culture, The PAAM-U Endowment Fund, and each local chapter.

All dues and funds will be received by the National Organization and disbursed to the appropriate fund. The National Organization will maintain an open book policy. Books will be open for review by any authorized representative of a Local Chapter 15 days following the end of each business quarter and remain open for review for 15 days. Independent auditing and reports will be contracted by the National Organization.

Strategy and Implementation Plan

The initial Implementation Plan is four stages, one year for each stage and each stage overlapping and on-going. The four stages are:

Stage 1. **Communication**
Stage 2. **Registration**
Stage 3. **Orientation**
Stage 4. **Implementation**

<u>**Explanations**</u>

Stage 1. Communication

The first year of communication consists of reading, studying, understanding and discussing all of the ideas contained in this book (manual). Each idea must be examined by the individual for agreement, disagreement, neutrality, the reason why and degree of each.

No person is expected to agree or believe everything in this book exactly as it is written. Total agreement or unity is not required for involvement. What is important is what you can find that can be used by you to help yourself and others grow in unity.

Discussion, debate, disagreement is healthy. We will struggle for agreement on as many areas as possible, and agree to disagree respectfully on all other areas. We must never lose sight of our overall goal--unity.

Stage 2. Registration

The registration process of filling out an application and officially participating in the creation of the organization begins as soon as the individual feels strongly enough about the cause, ideas, and materials to commit themselves. This can be done at any time but will officially begin one year after the communication effort has begun.

Stage 3. Orientation

Orientation is the actual meeting of people in groups and the communication of strategy for your group, city and state. Public notice of your group meeting, time, and place should be communicated so as to give all interested and appropriate parties an opportunity to participate. General application guidelines should be followed.

Stage 4. Implementation

This is the trial run and learning period for all aspects of The Code of Honor and Master Plan of Action to be implemented on a daily basis. Executive Committees and Advisory Boards interact with the total community.

POSITIVE AFRICAN AMERICAN MEN - UNITED, INC.
2133 12th Avenue North • Nashville, Tennessee 37208 • (615) 726-0203

Membership Application

Name _____

Address _____

_____

Phone _____   _____
        (Home)   (Work)

Date of Birth _____ Age _____   Sex ☐ Male   ☐ Female

Ethnic Classification: ☐ African American   ☐ Other, please name _____

Social Security Number _____-_____-_____

Affiliation: ☐ Member   ☐ Memorial   ☐ Participant   ☐ Supporter

☐ Patron: Name_____

Address_____

Payment Method: ☐ Annual   ☐ Semi-annual   ☐ Quarterly

Family covered by membership:

Names	Address	Age	D.O.B.	Relationship
_____	_____	___	_____	_____
_____	_____	___	_____	_____
_____	_____	___	_____	_____
_____	_____	___	_____	_____
_____	_____	___	_____	_____
_____	_____	___	_____	_____

PAAM-U 90

VI

NOTES AND VISIONS

WARNING

The topics in this section are separate and apart from PAAM-U. They represent only areas of discussion for African Americans. Each person is entitled to their own opinion in these areas. The author feels through discussion of ideas and their differences we grow as a people. From each discussion a strategy of dealing with future progress should emerge. This strategy should cross lines of division, as well as encourage and facilitate unity.

NOTES AND VISIONS

Notes represent subjects of concern and awareness. These subjects must be thought through and approached with new visions. Visions are our present positive realities or future realities, as we choose to create them.

To The African American Woman

This chapter is written to you from me. It expresses my thoughts, feelings, respect and love. This message is not intended to speak for anyone but myself.

PAAM-U and its Code of Honor cannot exist or fulfill itself without you and your cooperation and commitment. The purpose of this organization and its goal is based on recognition and respect for you, your history, and potential. I recognize you in every positive way conceivable. I recognize the tears, the pain, and the sacrifices you have made for your race in general, and for your sons and men in particular. You deserve help, assistance, and relief from responsibilities which are a man's place to shoulder. Part of my vision is that every women will have a positive African American man to assist her and that every African American child will have a PAAM-U man present to hold your hand and bond the child from birth to a strong man's touch and tenderness.

My vision is that those positive African American men will see, as I see that all children belong to us. That love is love regardless of its sources. The biological father is preferable, but a positive surrogate man is better than a negative natural father. My vision is that not one child will be without a positive mentor and male role model.

Please help us in your own way by allowing us access to your child. Help by cooperating with us in our efforts to pass on values that will produce men of which you will be proud. Trust us to do what is right.

Respect our wives and families and help us to keep those mates and families secure, so we can continue to help you without confusion at home. Wives please allow your husband to participate without confusion or insecurity at home. Each person who has a child will see that child claim a partner and reproduce. The person they choose could be a person your man helped to become a positive man or woman, or could be one he did not help, because you failed to provide encouragement.

There is no way for us to escape the reality that we are all in this together and we as a whole can only improve child by child, youth by youth, adult by adult. I hope that we can raise a flag of truce in dealing with our children. The reality of our situation will never allow the African American man to fulfill all his responsibilities on an economic, political, or religious level by a standard of judgment that compares us to our oppressor.

Allow us to give and please receive in a positive way, what we have to offer, which is beyond the control of our oppressor. Let us love our children and you.

<u>Help</u> us to regain our spiritual pride and dignity. <u>Help</u> us to make up to you the hundreds of years of rape and indignities you have had to suffer physically, emotionally, mentally and spiritually.

"Of What Value Is All The Wealth Of The World
If A Woman Must Sacrifice The Life Of Her First Born Son".

What About Our Girls and Young Women - The Unspoken Problem

One of the greatest unspoken problems our women face is the sexual abuse suffered as young girls. It appears countless numbers of young women from 9-18 are abused sexually by young boys, young men and men. Most of these attacks go unreported but leave deep psychological, emotional, and spiritual scars on our girls. The strong who learn how to physically fight, like a man, and to defend themselves, escape sexual penetration. The average and the weak are victimized. At this time there is no way to know how many adult women carry secrets of rape and physical attack which they have kept secret. It is unknown how many children have been born from a forced sexual act.

There can be no peace, positive communication, or unity among our people until these atrocities cease. Many of the problems couples experience, are the result of these unspoken and untreated incidents. Many of the negative attitudes held by our women are a result of legitimate grievances against male beast-like treatment.

Positive African American men must first establish a physical atmosphere, moral climate, and spiritual environment in which our young women are safe from sexual harassment and abuse as they develop into women.

The last issue in relationship to sexual abuse and harassment relates to the exploitation of young women by their parents. Too many reports of chemically dependent mothers encouraging or initiating sexual activity between men and their daughters for drug money are coming in, to be ignored. The emotional damage done to these children is irreparable and drain our race of potentially gifted people. Not only is this activity illegal but is a crime against humanity.

I strongly feel our young men need to be taught that they should not take anything from a girl or woman that she does not want them to have. Large amounts of time should be spent in our training programs on addressing positive ways for our males to relate to young women. Large amounts of time need to be spent sensitizing men to the damage they do when they use their power to hurt rather than help.

Principles of Womanhood

Positive African American Men-United will sponsor a training and mentorship program for girls and young women. This program will be constructed and administered by PAAM-U participating women. The purpose will be to provide a foundation and philosophy which compliments The Code of Honor and eight philosophies. The overall intent is that both our young men and young women grow and harmonize together for the unity of all.

The Traditional African American Church, The Exception and the Rule

For those of us who still look at the traditional African American Christian Church for solutions to social problems, let me mention this.

The primary purpose for the traditional African American Church is the recruitment of individuals to recognize Jesus Christ as their Lord and Savior. The recognition of Jesus Christ is the number one priority and rightly so. The second priority of the Church is worship and support of their ministry and rightly so. The third priority is the caring for individuals and family needs within the congregation--counseling, marrying, burying, and baptism. The forth purpose is the expansion and growth of the Church.

The social and cultural issues which apply specifically to African American people are of concern to the traditional church. However, those many courageous and gallant ministers who lead and sacrifice for our progress on social, political, and economic arenas represent the EXCEPTION RATHER THAN THE RULE for the traditional Church.

If one carefully looks at the religious challenge in the earlier paragraph. It is obvious the traditional Church has its work cut out for itself. It is a wonder we have as many committed Christian congregations as we do.

People often say to me "If we could get these churches together we could solve a lot of these problems". Getting churches united as a whole working group is not going to happen now, or in the future. African American traditional ministers and churches can barely work with unity among their own congregation and denominations. Interdenominational work and cooperation is impossible for an extended period of time.

Please give our Christian churches a break and recognize they need help also. The Code of Honor provides ministers and churches with a cultural base to fulfill Christian teaching. Remember, Jesus had the benefit of Jewish culture and tradition for his original ministry to Jews and the Jewish culture.

However, let us encourage the Black Church to work with integrity. If ministers within the various denominations, sects, and individual churches can just accomplish one task within themselves, it will help our people a great deal.

Jesus, as the Bible states, was a Jew. Jews of that period were from a semitic tribe. There were no blond haired, blue eyed Jews. The Bible states that Jesus had skin the color of bronze and hair like lambs wool. If our churches can portray Jesus and his followers as semitic Jews instead of Europeans, it would help our self esteem. Please remove the stained glass and portraits of the European Jew and replace them with the actual African, but so called Middle East Jew, of 2000 years ago.

African American Unity Prayer

Our Creator
we pray for unity
under the direction of your spirit and will,
to work, think and act in a positive way.
To honor, respect and protect
our women, children, elders and men
through our love, commitment, guidance, time and support.

We pray
that you lead us in promoting sincere brotherhood
by our proudly befriending and standing shoulder to shoulder
with the positive people of our race and the world.
Amen.

We ask that all African American gatherings of two or more recite this prayer at the beginning of each meeting, until we are united.

Brotherhood

Unity as positive African American men, as brothers, and allies for the betterment of our people is essential. There can be no peace or compromise with negativity. Those of us who love our people beyond our own personal gratification are candidates for this fraternity.

Those of us who have studied or lived through it know the negative forces, which rejoice at our weaknesses, will stop at nothing to continue the destruction of our people. We all know that everyone in this race is not automatically for this race and its fulfillment.

Internal strife and discord is our enemy. Being swayed into the arena of difference, which comes from political, monetary, or religious disagreements is our enemy. To love, support, and mentor other African American males who are committed to positive action and thought is our duty.

Note from the Klan[4]

The following is the contents of a letter placed on the bed of a young Afro-American incarcerated in the Chicago city jail. Please take a minute to reflect upon the severity of this statement.

The Ku Klux Klan would like to take this time to salute and congratulate all Gang Bangers, all Alcohol Drinking Abusers, and all Drug Users for the slaughter of over 4,000 black people since 1975. You are doing a marvelous job. Keep killing each other for nothing. The streets are still not yours...it is ours. You killing each other for our property. You are killing what could be future black doctors, lawyers, and businessmen that we won't have to compete with. And the good thing about it is that you are killing youth. So we won't have to worry about you niggers in generations to come. We would further like to thank all the judges who have oversentenced those niggers to prison.

We are winning again. Pretty soon, we will be able to go back to raping your women. Because all the men will be gone.

So you Gang Bangers, Alcohol Drinking Abusers and Drug Users, keep up the good work. We love to read about drive-by shootings. We love to hear how many niggers get killed over the weekends. We can tolerate the niggers with jungle fever (for now)...because that further breaks down the race.

To all Gang Bangers, Alcohol Drinking Abusers and Drug Users across the world: We don't love you niggers, but we can appreciate you. You are doing a wonderful job in eliminating the black race. Without the men...your women cannot reproduce...Unless of

---

[4]The author of this letter is unknown. There is no verification of the author or their actual affiliation with the Klan. This letter was received by Sidney Wingfield through the unofficial network of African Americans working in the criminal justice systems. March 1992.

course, we do it for them. Then we have successfully eliminated a race, thanks to your help and commitment to killing each other.

If most of you nigger Gang Bangers, Alcohol Drinking Abusers, and Drug Users cannot read this letter. It is OK. Go pull a trigger and kill a nigger.
Thank you.

The Oppressor/The Enemy--Ignorance, Fear, Indifference, and Disunity

We tend to think of the oppressor as the White race in general and the White male specifically. This like any generality is true, but not accurate. There is no doubt that, historically, the White race can be viewed with disdain for the horrors perpetuated in every corner of the world. However, the mentality of greed, selfishness and materialism are universal. Whites have been more efficient, organized, and unified, but not original.

It is too easy for us to blame all our problems on the White race. History is clear that Whites have had to struggle within themselves for freedom. The oppressive feudal systems of royalty and aristocracy sparked the Revolution that founded the United States, basically White against White. The horrors of the industrial revolution with children chained to machines in factories produced the Child Labor Law movement. White people exploiting White people. Police and law enforcement agencies from the beginning of European and American History were formed to protect White people from White people. The struggle for protection and justice has been, and remains, an internal issue for the White race. It has been the positive element of the White race which have moved them forward and assisted African Americans, just as the positive element of our race has moved us forward.

For the record, let it be clearly stated that each person must be judged by their own individual potential and merit. Elitism, sexism, and racism are negatives which have no place in our thinking.

Even though we live in an elitist, sexist, and racist society, this does not automatically condemn every beneficiary of that society as an elitist, sexist, or racist. Nor does this automatically exempt every victim of oppression from being an elitist, sexist, or racist.

As we try to analyze our enemy and oppressor, we all search for simple answers and generalizations. **We must be constantly aware that the enemy and oppressor is a mind set and negative value system. This negative mentality can dominate the actions and behavior of any person regardless of color.** Our struggle for liberation is both internal and external. At this point in our history, statistics prove we are more destructive to ourselves than any external force.

Let us begin at the beginning with unity.

Dialogue With White America

PAAM-U is exactly what it's name is--positive. Our intention is to create and maintain positive links to communication and work with the positive elements of White America. We recognize and honor the lives lost, bloodshed and sacrifices made by sincere Whites throughout our history in America. Those Whites who can share and support our goals and aspirations are welcome to contribute what they have to offer.

Our relationship to you is with the understanding that your interaction and assistance are under our direction and control. Even though in some cases your resources and experience may be greater than ours, it is only through our own leadership and experiences that we can grow and maintain a solid cultural base of self determination and pride. Those truly positive Whites will respect the reality of the African American experience as unique, and accept our leadership.

The unspoken issue that will cause the greatest difficulty from both races is the issue of our blood relationship. Both races know, whether they choose to admit it or not, that African Americans have European blood running thought their veins as well as African. This is true, if not in total fact but in principal, from the years of rape of our women endured during slavery. This issue is not intended to be approached from a negative view of the past but a positive view for the future. It is intended to bring to light and deal with the reality of the relationship between European Americans and African Americans is first and foremost a blood relationship of people who are actually related to each other, regardless of the circumstances. When both groups can accept and positively deal with the reality of our blood relationship, the races will have one bridge built and one less excuse to be polarized.

The greatest assistance we can hope to obtain from positive White American is the control and containment of the negative elements of your race who seek to exploit or hurt our people in any way they can.

A superficial survey of our history shows that we are linked not only by blood, but by destiny to the progress of this country and White America. We are without a doubt the first line of defense for any negative elements that may befall White America in the future, as exemplified by the current drug problem, first created to destroy Black America.

We welcome and encourage your suggestions and support and encourage those of you who support this program and its purpose to contact me. I also recognize in many ways the oppressor is as much a victim of their oppression as the oppressed. True liberation must be with the intent of addressing all victims.

A Special Note to the White Woman's Liberation Movement

I've only met two kinds of women, oppressed and more oppressed. The difference between the two is that the oppressed woman realizes that she is oppressed and that sexism, racism, and elitism are merely different fingers on the same hand. While the more oppressed woman sees no similarity and separates all things. The feminine aspect of your history throughout the world has been first for compassion, first for peace, first for sensitivity, first for health, first for children, and first for love. The world would be in a much worse condition if it existed without your influences and contributions.

As we pursue our struggles for liberation, I ask that you remember African American men and boys are on record and have been steadfastly proven to be the most vulnerable and powerless group of people in the world today. No victory over this group can have meaning or merit. Let us respect each other. The struggle you face is not merely men against women, but our common enemy is power over the powerless. It is ignorance and fear over knowledge and truth. We must recognize that all people are people first, women and men, White and Black, rich and poor, second, third or fourth.

To The Hispanic Communities

My understanding of the Hispanic communities in the United States is that it is diverse. The term Hispanics is used to cover all Spanish speaking or Latin people, Mexican, Puerto Ricans, Cubans, Chicanos, etc.[5] Within the varied Hispanic cultural are people of all three major race groups: Caucasian, Mongolian and Negroid.[6]

My focus is on our common challenge: the development of the God-given talents and abilities within every child born. PAAM-U has attempted to set forth a Code of Honor for men which is universal to all men, regardless of race and cultural classification. PAAM-U is open and willing to stand shoulder with positive men of our race and the world.

The sharing of information and cooperation to develop the total human potential is required of us.

Our posture toward the Hispanic community is one of human respect and shared common social challenges. This work is available, and positive representatives of the Hispanic communities who feel it will benefit them in any way.

We are open to Hispanic volunteers who wish to teach or tutor Spanish, Portuguese, history, and culture of specific Hispanic cultures.

To The Asian Pacific American Communities and People

Positive African American Men United will encourage and facilitate deeper understanding and communication between our peoples. The recognition of your diverse

---

[5] Fred Ortiz (El Paso Times No Date)

[6] Guadalupe Silva (El Paso Times March 27, 1988)

cultures, languages, and history is of importance to us as we lay the beginning, formal foundation of a culture within a culture.

As our organization progresses, the door will open for those who wish to teach history, culture, or a language of their ancestral country or culture to African American people.

To The American Jewish People

This text has used the Jewish culture, religion, and traditions as positive examples and models for the building of African American culture. The foundation of Black history from the beginning of slavery has been rooted in the Old Testament and Jewish history.

We hope to act as a positive vehicle for increased communication and improved relations. Any perceived error or misrepresentation of Jewish culture is unintentional and open to correction. As our organization progresses, the door will be open for those who wish to teach history, culture, or language of their culture to African American people.

To The Native American

Positive African American Men-United extends its hand in friendship and support. If there is anything I or my people can do to assist you in any way, please do not hesitate to ask. We recognize that large numbers of African American are mixed with Native Americans by blood. We honor our blood relationship to the many tribes throughout the United States and Canada.

We as a people formally apologize and ask for your forgiveness of our misguided involvement in your people's oppression.

You are welcome to use any part of this work which will benefit your people. We recognize the diversity of Native Americans and the internal struggles which divide tribe within tribe. We are open to education, information, and training from any of your people who wish to teach.

To Our African Brothers and Sisters

To speak of a united Africa to an African is to speak of a difficult, if not impossible, challenge. My African brothers tell me that Africa's division of language, tribal cultures, and customs would make unity virtually impossible. We as African Americans realize how close we are and yet so far apart.

It appears African Americans with a common racial heritage are separated by culture and custom as much as any other group or country of native Africans from a unity.

Our organization wishes to recognize the diversity of African people and open the door for the appreciation and teaching of specific countries, cultures, and tribes. As our organization progresses, the door will be open for those who wish to teach history, cultures, or language to African American people.

America's Chosen People

We are uniquely American in that all the blood of all the races of the world flows through our veins. From the darkest blue black to the palest albino, our people exemplify the melting pot intended by God, for America and the homogenous world. We are America's chosen people.

Born out of slavery for humility and historical necessity, it was intended that the last should be first. First in humility, first in love, first in spiritual bonds with God.

Within us are all the truths that have existed since the beginning of mankind, from the heights of intelligence to the depths of blind ignorance. It is our task to develop the positive and control the downward spiral of the negative. The extra mile must be walked with our enemy and friends, for only positive action and thought can bring about the change our people need and the world must have. Our history is the world, our heritage is the world, our future is the world.

We Are African European Americans: The Hard and Painful Truth

Colored, Negro, Afro-American, Black, African American, and Afrikan American. As we continue to struggle with our identity, the time and world go on. We see in our midst, generation after generation worse off than the first and each less qualified to deal with the ever-increasing pressure of a racist, oppressive, genocidal American society.

Yet, each answer and each definition of who we are seems to give less power and unity to our people as a whole and each of us as individuals. Why? We are all aware of the symptoms manifested by an oppressed people: low self-esteem, self-hatred, the love, envy and desire to be like our oppressor.

Perhaps all of our definitions fall short of our complete heritage and the truth. Perhaps we are in conflict with the whole truth. Perhaps we only want to see that part of ourselves and our history that validates our innocence and pride. Perhaps we as a people act much like an individual when examining who we are. Life would be very simple and beautiful if we could have all things both ways--money without work, fame without development of talent--have our cake and eat it too. Fortunately, we live in an organized physical universe governed by basic laws and principles. The most supreme law is cause and effect. If one throws a rock it will return to earth in complete harmony with the physical principle we classify as gravity. If one goes into a gym and puts forth the effort needed to conquer the objects of resistance or weights in that gym, one will become stronger. Usually, for unused muscles, this effort to overcome resistance or weight is accompanied by pain, or the body's natural reaction to change and growth by force. We all know the cliche, "no pain no gain".

This analogy and cliche also directly relate to our people and our ongoing efforts to redefine ourselves. We basically fear the pain that accompanies the truth about ourselves and our complete heritage. From that fear of pain, comes our conscious denial of the truth. A person or race of people who consciously denies that which they subconsciously know is the truth, or who openly denies that which they privately admit is in conflict with themselves. The inside truth is in conflict with the outside denial.

Let me explore for a brief period the conflict of truth that we all know exists. These truths are simple and not debatable:

Fact: African people were kidnapped from their Motherland and forced into slavery.

Fact: Both Europeans and Africans participated in perpetrating this crime.

Fact: The descendants of those kidnapped victims openly acknowledge Europeans as perpetrators of slavery.

Fact: The systematic rape of African women by Europeans was continuous, consistent, extensive, and common practice.

Fact: The children conceived by this systematic rape had as much European blood in their veins as African.

Fact: The perpetrators of this rape legally and culturally denied their blood relationship.

Fact: The African European blood relationship exists whether it is acknowledged or denied.

Fact: The children of African European descendants openly denied this blood relationship, while privately acknowledging it.

Fact: The African European off-spring have reacted to rejection in a normal way by passively accepting that rejection and aggressively acknowledging that which acknowledges them, Africa and the African cultural heritage tradition.

As a race of people, we are dysfunctional culturally due to this passive public denial. I would compare it to the child of an unwed mother whose companion denies his paternity. When the mother tells the child who his or her father is and the father rejects the child as his son or daughter, the child rejects the father. Is there anyone who hasn't seen or heard of the bitter child who says he has no father. The rejection is too difficult to acknowledge so the child rejects that which rejects him or her. As natural as this is to understand, the reality of its effects on the child or race of people is devastating, functionally.

In cases like this most clinicians recommend therapy, and ideally, as many individuals participating as possible. A dialogue between the child, mother and father is ideal, where all anger is expressed, all sides of the story explored and mutual relationships of love and trust begin. In our world today, the ideal is rare. When this child reaches adulthood and is unable to achieve the goals and success it desires because of unresolved problems in his childhood, treatment and wholeness can still be obtained if sought after. The mother and father may both have passed but there are some things that can be done to resolve the situation. The first is acknowledgment and acceptance of the truth. The second is looking for the positive within what appears negative.

We as a people can continue to define, redefine, and rename ourselves, but there can be no peace or progress until we accept and look for the positive in our true heritage. We are, in reality, <u>African European American</u> people.

No matter how we struggle to deny this, the facts are unquestionable. No matter how much we choose to uplift the victim and place blame on the rapist, his relationship to the child is fact. There is no so-called African-American who does not have some European blood in their veins. There is no aspect of our culture, Black or White, that can honestly and openly deny the reality of our heritage. This is who we are; this is our heritage; and this is our true name. We are African European Americans and this is a hard and painful truth to face.

I know there will be some people who will read this and will say I have no European traits and all of my physical characteristics are African. Therefore, I reject your statement that all of us have some European blood in our veins. My reply to this is look at your mate or your children. If you don't have European physical characteristics, I guarantee you the man or woman you sleep with, or have slept with, does, and the children you produce, or the children they produce, will reflect African European traits.

If we as a people ever hope to eliminate the pain, suffering, and failure we see daily in the news media and with our own eyes, or the pain we experience personally, we must first know and accept ourselves and who we are before we can improve ourselves and our condition. Let us begin at the beginning.

"....And you will know the truth, and the truth will make you free..."

John 8:32

The Elderly

There is no greater crime in America than to be African American, old, poor, and without loving relatives. I had the opportunity to work for several years as a medical social worker for three health care agencies. Most of the cases I handled were elderly persons who had lost their Medicaid benefits due to their failure to renew benefits once each year as required by the law.

The way the system works is a green Medicaid card is sent once a month. This card allows the individual to purchase medicine at the pharmacy for free or minimal costs. If the individual does not have a card, by law the pharmacist cannot dispense their prescription.

All of the individuals on my case load had already been off their medication for 30 to 60 days before a referral was made. In most cases, the renewal form was discarded by the patient because they did not understand what the form was for. A combination of poor eyesight, ageing, senility, declining health, fine print, and lack of a caring person to read mail was the culprit.

In many cases, pharmacies would fill prescriptions or give medication at their own expense to aide these people until their new cards came in. Most of the time neither the patient, pharmacist nor doctor was aware that the patient had been terminated from the program.

Usually it took 30 - 60 days for someone to realize the patients had not renewed their eligibility and 30 days to correct the situation. In many experiences patients who missed or were irregular with their medication for 30 - 60 days were hospitalized within 12 to 18 months. Patients who missed or were irregular with medication for up to 90 days usually died within 12 - 18 months.

My practical solution to this problem was color coded Medicaid cards with the next to the last card colored yellow and the final card red. All the pharmacists surveyed said they would be more than glad to check with and assist patients completing forms for continuous coverage.

The Greatest Outrage

The greatest outrage in our lack of unity is that our elderly people are the primary targets for crime in inner cities. There is no more cowardly act than victimizing a defenseless person. Robbery and injury of the elderly result in death too often. One of the goals of PAAM-U is to eliminate the victimization of the elderly by whatever legal means necessary. We will not tolerate our mothers and fathers used as prey for cowardly criminals. We will protect our defenseless people.

One of the major responsibilities of PAAM-U will be the protection and transportation of the elderly through high crime areas. There will be a standing reward for information leading to the apprehension and conviction for any crime against our elderly or their property. My vision is that PAAM-U will allow no elderly person to be alone or defenseless.

Jobs and Unemployment

Work Force 2000

Today, the future appears brighter in potential for our children than it has been for us. In the coming century, studies state the profile of the all-American worker will change. The profile change is the result of two things: one, the declining birth rate for White America, and two, the demand for people to fill needed jobs in all areas of labor, and lower management.

The profile of the all American worker will change from blond haired blue eyed White male to African American, Hispanic and Asian. Competition will move more to merit than race. As a people, this seems to be our greatest task to qualify our children for jobs across the board through education. Although change is coming soon, things will remain the same. As in every area, we have to be twice as good and work twice as hard for the same money and less recognition.

This aspect will stay with us. We also must face the pressure of Asian and Hispanic prejudice. One thing is perfectly clear, all race groups have their prejudices, and no one in the world wants to be classified with the American Black person.

Unity is called for to educate our children. The problems of unemployment as we have known it are not over for our children. Now, let us do what we need to do and prepare them for their future.

Sisters and Brothers Without Fathers or Mothers

Most African American people are prepared for negative stereotypes and personal stories surrounding males and father figures. In our culture it is acceptable and standard practice for the man to be cast in the role of the bad guy.

Few people who have experienced it will acknowledge or talk about the pain felt when it is their mother who is the bad guy.

Motherhood in our culture is held in such high esteem that the acceptance by children of their mother's faults is rare. Denial and secrecy run highest in mother-child issues. In our culture for a person to speak ill of, or joke, signify, or play the dozens about another person's mother could, and in many cases does, lead to violence. In many cases, the person is angered not by the joke but by the resemblance of some truth.

Everyone wants to love their mother. Everyone wants to think their mom is the best mom. Historically, in our culture "mom" has been held in high esteem because she did not abandon you as fathers have. She was there for you and if not her, grandmother took over and symbolized the mother figure.

For those who have experienced abandonment, betrayal, rejection, drug abuse, prostitution, promiscuity, mental or emotional illness, suicide or death of your mother, PAAM-U understands this paradox and is here to support children and adults whose mother/child experiences may be less than desirable. We are also here to support mothers who want to be better mothers to their sons and daughters.

VII

TERMS

TERMS

African American:	A term used to describe those Americans whose racial heritage is directly from Africa and the people of color from the African continent (see race). In this text African American is used to describe the unique culture of Black Americans.
Befriend:	To be truthful, honest, considerate, supportive, and respectful of another person.
Black:	(1) Beautiful (2) a color (3) the color used to describe people from the Negroid racial classification. (see race). Black people in America have also been known as Negro, Nigra, Color, and people of color. In this text Black is used to describe race and African American is used to describe culture.
Code:	(1) Rules which govern a person's conduct and behavior. (2) A system by which communication is made secret to all but those who know the system.
Commitment:	To obligate your actions and behavior to an agreed upon goal or result.
Complete:	Whole. To finish what one begins to the best of ones ability.
Courage:	The ability to think and act in a positive manner in spite of any fears you may have.
Dirty Work:	Work which is not considered pleasant either because of physical, mental or emotional conditions.
Duty:	Specific thoughts, actions and behavior that persons are obligated to fulfill and complete by God, nature, chance or circumstance.
Family:	Those people you are related to through love or blood line.
Goals:	Specific objectives that you are willing to work towards until completion.
God:	A term used to describe the higher power beyond complete human understanding. The source of all things. The primary cause of all things.
Guidance:	Positive thoughtful actions which improves a person's life and moves them toward positive goals.

Terms (continued)

Hard Work:	Physical or mental work that challenges a person's physical, mental or emotional ability to complete.
Home:	Where a person lives or where a person's heart is. Where you feel you belong.
Honor:	(1) Living, working, performing one's duty and completing one's responsibility as a man or woman by choosing positive thoughts, actions and behavior which allow a person to respect themselves, and when recognized by others deserve respect and admiration. (2) To act and think with courage using logic that is spiritually correct and true. (3) Acting towards and treating others the way one would want to be treated.
Kwanzaa:	An African American holiday that celebrates our rich African culture and heritage. The seven principles of Kwanzaa are based on the Nguzo Saba which benefits the family, the community and mankind. The seven principles are unity, self-determination, collective work and responsibility, cooperative economics, purpose, creativity, and faith
Knowledge:	Information and experiences you have learned and can apply to work or life wisely.
Learn:	The ability to take in information and experiences until you understand how to apply it to work or life wisely.
Love:	A level of awareness and concern for another person's well being and progress beyond your own benefit.
Man:	(1) Mind. (2) A fully developed male who actively works to grow in his relationship to God, family, race and the world. (3) A male who works to the best of his ability to fulfill his duties and responsibilities in life. (4) A male who acts with courage in the face of fear and doubt.
Mankind:	A term used to describe the human race.
Master:	(1) To have complete knowledge and understanding of oneself in a given area of study. (2) To overcome obstacles or barriers between a person and their goals.
Pledge:	To promise, to commit oneself to specific actions or behavior.
Positive:	Plus, good, better, best, helpful, asset, light, knowledge. An attitude and behavior. A plus sign (+) in science, mathematics or physics.

Terms (continued)

Promote: To advance an idea, person or thing in a positive light.

Proudly: To be unashamed, to have pride in. Attitude and behavior.

Pursue: To go after with a desire to achieve.

Race: European classification of people by color and physical features or geographical origin. The three classifications are Negroid, Mongoloid, and Caucasoid all of which overlap.

Respect: Positive treatment or attitude of/and for yourself and others.

Responsibility: Action, attitude and duty that is yours alone to perform for yourself and others.

School: A designated building or place where information is available and people strive to learn. Any place where one grows in knowledge and/or wisdom.

Study: To observe and review with the goal of learning.

Support: To help mentally, emotionally, physically, financially, spiritually.

Tasks: Any goal or objective which requires mental or physical work to complete or overcome.

Time: The orderly division of our planet's rotation around the sun and its rotation on its axis. Its separation by day and night by seconds, minutes, hours, days, months, seasons and years.

Trust: Faith placed in an individual, thing, rule or principal that may or may not be supported by history.

Universal: (1) Beyond the limits of social, legal or traditional restraints which limit thinking. Unlimited Thought. (2) That which can be understood, used, appreciated, produced and/or experienced by all persons. Examples: art, music, food, laughter, love, hunger, fear, ignorance, excitement, life and death.

Work: (1) Physical, mental, emotional or spiritual energy put forth to achieve a desired goal or result. (2) Directly connected to a man's feeling of value and self-worth.

World: The planet earth, your family and total environment.

ABOUT THE AUTHOR

Sidney Wingfield was born in Chicago, Illinois May 21, 1946 and separated from his mother and biological family at birth. Sidney grew up in the foster home of William and Sarah Bass on Chicago's south side community, Morgan Park.

When Sidney was 11 years old his foster father died, and he assumed responsibility as the man of the house for his foster mother. Sidney's foster mother became an invalid by the time he reached 14, and she fought off death until one month after his graduation from high school at age 17½.

Sidney was drafted in the United States Army at age 19, during the Vietnam conflict. He served two years and was honorably discharged in 1968.

Sidney has been a student and teacher of world religions, behavioral sciences, cultural anthropology, philosophy, theology, and metaphysics for over 20 years. He is a certified Master Social Worker, and for the past 10 years has worked in a range of positions with the Juvenile Court System, currently as a Program Director. He has counseled and worked in the areas of chemical dependency, juvenile delinquency, foster care, child protective service, child advocacy, geriatrics, community and family social work.

Sidney's academic background is a Bachelor of Arts degree from Scarritt College for Christian Workers, with a dual concentration in Behavioral Sciences and World Religions, and a Master of Science in Social Work degree, earned at the University of Tennessee at Nashville. Sidney feels any success he has enjoyed is due to the blessing of God and the efforts of foster parents, teachers, community center staff, ministers, policemen, drill sergeants, and helping professionals, and any faults or shortcomings are all his own.